BPMN Pocket Reference

A Practical Guide To The International Business Process Model And Notation Standard

BPMN Version 2.0

Kenneth J Sherry

First Published 2012
By Admaks Publishing
www.admaks.com

Copyright © Admaks Publishing

All rights reserved. No part of this publication may be reproduced, stored in or introduced into a retrieval system, or transmitted, in any form, or by any means electronic, mechanical or other means, now known or hereafter invented, including xerography, photocopying and recording, without the prior written permission of the publisher.

This book is sold subject to the condition that it shall not, by of trade or otherwise, be lent, resold, hired out, or otherwise circulated without the publishers prior consent in any form of binding or cover other than that which it is published and without a similar condition including this condition being imposed on the subsequent purchaser.

First edition 2012

Table of Contents

Introduction   **8**
    Business Process Model and Notation (BPMN)   8

Activity Notations   **9**
    Task Notation   9
    Collapsed Sub-process Notation   9
    None / Unspecified   10
    Loop Activity   10
    Multi-Instance Characteristics   10
    Multi-Instance Parallel Activity   11
    Multi-Instance Sequential Activity   11
    Compensation   12
    Ad-Hoc Sub-process   12
    Expanded Sub-process   12

Task Types   **14**
    Abstract Task   14
    Send Task   14
    Receive Task   15
    Send and Receive Task Example   16
    Receive Task Initiating A Process   17
    Human Interactions Tasks   19
    Manual Task   19
    User Task   19
    Business Rule Task   20
    Script Task   20
    Service Task   20
    Process Without Task Types Example   21
    Using Task Types In A BPD   22
    Process With Task Types Example   23

Call Activities   **24**
    Call Activity   24
    Manual Call Activity   24
    User Call Activity   25
    Business Call Activity   25
    Script Call Activity   25

Call Activity Calling A Process	25
Call Activity Expanded	26

Connectors 27

Sequence Flows	27
Conditional Flows	27
Default Sequence Flows	27
Sequence flow Example	28
Message Flows	28
Association	29
Directional Association	29
Bi-directional Association	30
Conversational link	30

Messages 31

Initiating Message	31
Non-Initiating Message	31
Messages With Choreography Tasks	32

Conversations 33

Conversation Node	33
Sub-Conversation Node	35
Global Call Conversation	36
Collaboration Call Conversation	36

Choreography 37

Choreography Task	37
None Or Unspecified Choreography Task	38
Choreography Task – Loop	38
Choreography Task - Sequential Multi Instance	38
Choreography Task - Parallel Multi Instance	39
Sub-Choreography Elements	40
Sub-Choreography - Collapsed	40
None Or Unspecified Sub-Choreography - Collapsed	41
Sub-Choreography Loop - Collapsed	41
Sub-Choreography Sequential Multi-Instance –Collapsed	41
Sub-Choreography Parallel Multi Instance - Collapsed	42
Choreography Sequence Flow	43
Choreography Example	44
Choreography Within A Collaboration Example	45

Artefacts 46

BPMN artefact elements	46
Data Association	46
Data Objects	46
Data Input	47
Data Output	47
Data Object Examples	48
Group Notation	49
Annotations	49
Data Store	49

Gateways 50

Exclusive Gateways	50
Data-Based XOR	51
Exclusive Event-Based Gateways	52
Merge Event-Based XOR Gateway	53
Fork Event-Based XOR Gateway	54
Parallel Gateways	55
Inclusive Gateways	57
Complex Gateways	59
Complex Decision Gateways	59
Complex Merge Gateways	60

Process Pools and Swimlanes 61

Process Pool	61
Multi Instance Pool	62
Swimlanes	62
Communication Between Pools	63
Pools And Swimlanes Example	64
Black And White Box Pools	65

Start Events 66

Interrupt And Non-interrupt Start Events	66
None Or Unspecified Start Event	66
Message Start Event	67
Timer Start Event	68
Conditional Start Event	69
Multiple Start Event	70
Parallel Multiple Start Event	71

End Events 72

None or Unspecified End Event	72
Message End Event	73

Multiple End Event	74
Terminate End Event	75

Inline Intermediate Events   76

None Or Unspecified Intermediate Event	77
Message Intermediate Catching Event	78
Message Intermediate Throwing Event	78
Timer Intermediate Catching Event	80
Conditional Intermediate Catching Event	81
Multiple Intermediate Catching Event	82
Multiple Intermediate Throwing Event	83
Parallel Multiple Intermediate Catching Event	85
Intermediate Links	86

Boundary Intermediate Events   87

Interrupt And Non-interrupt Boundary Intermediate Events	87
Message Intermediate Boundary Event	88
Timer Intermediate Boundary Event	91
Conditional Intermediate Boundary Event	93
Multiple Intermediate Boundary Event	95
Parallel Multiple Intermediate Boundary Events	98

Escalation Events   100

Escalation Start Event	100
Escalation Intermediate Boundary Events	100
Escalation Intermediate Throwing Event	101
Escalation End Event	101
Escalation Events Example 1	102
Escalation Events Example 2	103

Signal Events   104

Signal Start Event	104
Signal Intermediate Catching Event	105
Signal Intermediate Throwing Event	105
Signal End Event	105
Signal Intermediate Event Example 1	106
Signal Intermediate Boundary Event	107
Signal Intermediate Event Example 2	108

Cancel Events   109

Cancel End Event	109
Cancel Intermediate Boundary Event	109

Cancel Events Example	110

Error Events   **111**

Error Start Event	111
Error Intermediate Boundary Event	112
Error End Event	112
Error Event Example 1	113
Error Event Example 2	114

Compensation Events   **115**

Compensation Start Event	115
Compensation Intermediate Boundary Event	115
Compensation Activity Example	116
Compensation Intermediate Throwing Event	117
Compensation End Event Throwing	117
Compensation Example 1	118
Compensation Example 2	119

Collapsed Event Sub-Processes   **120**

Message Event Sub-Processes	121
Timer Event Sub-Processes	121
Conditional Event Sub-Processes	122
Multiple Event Sub-Processes	122
Parallel Multiple Event Sub-Processes	123
Escalation Event Sub-Processes	123
Signal Event Sub-Processes	124
Error Event Sub-Process	124
Compensation Event Sub-Process	124

Further Reading   **125**

Introduction

Business Process Model and Notation (BPMN)

The object of BPMN is to support business process management, for both technical users and business users, by providing a notation that is intuitive and able to represent complex process semantics to the business community as a whole.

BPMN provides a simple means of communicating business process information to other business users, process implementers, customers and suppliers alike.

The intent of BPMN is to standardise business process modelling with an open source graphical notation for specifying business processes in a business process model.

BPMN was first released as Business Process Modelling Notation in May 2004 version 1.0.

The present version 2.0 was released March 2011 as the Business Process Model and Notation.

The BPMN specification was conceived by representatives across the global business modelling community, to define a graphical notation and the semantics of collaboration diagrams, process diagrams, and choreography diagrams.

Activity Notations

An activity is defined as a piece of work that is performed within a business process. There are two types of notations used, Task and Sub-process.

Tasks are activities performed at a specific point in the process sequence.

Sub-processes are containers of groups of tasks and can also contain further Sub-processes.

Each Task or Sub-process performs some type of work on incoming information, therefore producing an output.

Tasks and Sub-process can have different markers depending on the type of activity to be performed; unspecified, multi-Instance, loop, compensation or Ad-Hoc.

It is feasible to create different combinations of markers to perform different activities but the loop and multi-instance cannot be used for the same activity.

Task Notation

The *Task* symbol is shown as a rectangle with rounded corners drawn with a thin line.

Collapsed Sub-process Notation

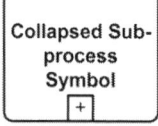

The *Collapsed Sub-process* symbol is shown as a rectangle with rounded corners drawn with a thin line containing a plus sign (+) in the centre bottom.

None / Unspecified

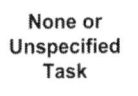

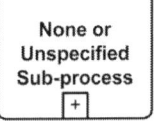

A *None / Unspecified* Task or *Collapsed Sub-process* are the most commonly used notations. Their only requirement is to perform the described activity.

Loop Activity

A *Loop* symbol is shown as a circle with an arrow on the end placed in the centre bottom of the rectangle.

The *Loop Task* or *Collapsed Sub-process* notations are used to show that the same specific Task or Sub-process is performed a number of times, before continuing the sequence flow.

Multi-Instance Characteristics

The Multi-instance Task or Collapsed Sub-process may execute in parallel or be sequential.

Either an expression is used to specify or calculate the desired number of instances or a data driven setup is used.

If a data input is specified, the number of items in the data collection determines the number of activity instances.

This data input can be produced by an input data Association.

The loop characteristic markers (Loop, Multi-Instance - Parallel and Multi-Instance - Sequential) are mutually exclusive markers and only one of them can be depicted on a single activity.

Multi-Instance Parallel Activity

A *Multi-Instance Parallel* symbol is shown as three parallel vertical lines in the centre bottom of the element.

| Multi-Instance Parallel Task ||| | Multi-Instance Parallel Sub-process ||| + |

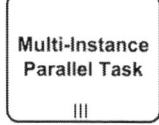

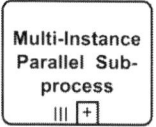

The *Multi-Instance Parallel Task* or *Collapsed Sub-process* describes multiple parallel activities or multiple sub-processes. They are used when two or more of the same Tasks or Sub-processes are performed simultaneously.

Multi-Instance Sequential Activity

A *Multi-Instance Sequential* symbol is shown as three parallel horizontal lines in the centre bottom of the element.

| Multi-Instance Sequential Task ≡ | Multi-Instance Sequential Sub-process ≡ + |

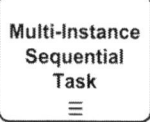

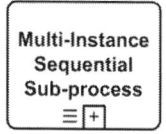

The *Multi-Instance Sequential Task* or *Collapsed Sub-process* describes multiple sequential activities or multiple sub-processes.

They are used when two or more of the same Tasks or Sub-processes are performed, one after the other.

Compensation

A *Compensation* symbol is represented by two triangles pointing left.

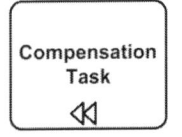

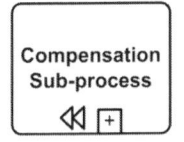

```
┌─────────────┐   ┌─────────────┐
│Compensation │   │Compensation │
│    Task     │   │ Sub-process │
│     ◁◁      │   │    ◁◁ +     │
└─────────────┘   └─────────────┘
```

The *Compensation Task* or *Collapsed Compensation Sub-process* are only required when a specified Task or Sub-process needs to be undone (unwound).

Ad-Hoc Sub-process

An *Ad-Hoc* sub-process symbol is represented by a wavy line next to the plus sign in the centre bottom of the symbol.

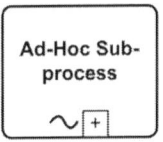

```
┌─────────────┐
│ Ad-Hoc Sub- │
│   process   │
│             │
│    ∼ +      │
└─────────────┘
```

The *Ad-Hoc Collapsed Sub-process* describes a situation that does not have a pre-defined sequence flow and is therefore considered Ad-Hoc

An Ad-Hoc task is not specified but the possibility of an Ad-Hoc sub-process as a loop is conceivable.

Expanded Sub-process

An *Expanded Sub-process* is shown as a separate diagram. The tasks, sub-processes, decisions and events, required to perform the activity are depicted inside the expanded sub-process.

If the collapsed sub-process has an activity symbol, this is shown within the expanded sub-process diagram

There are 5 types of *Expanded Sub-process* notations

- None / Unspecified
- Multi-Instance
- Loop
- Compensation
- Ad-Hoc

Expanded Sub-process Example

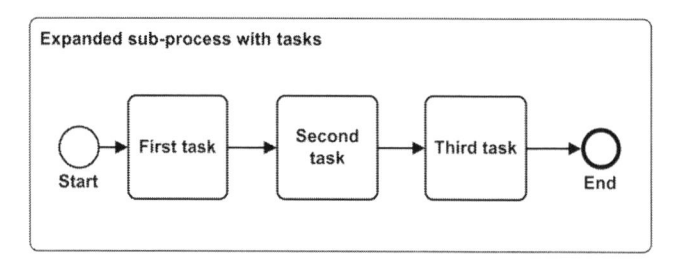

Expanded sub-process with tasks

Start → First task → Second task → Third task → End

Expanded Sub-processes can also include further sub-processes for granularity.

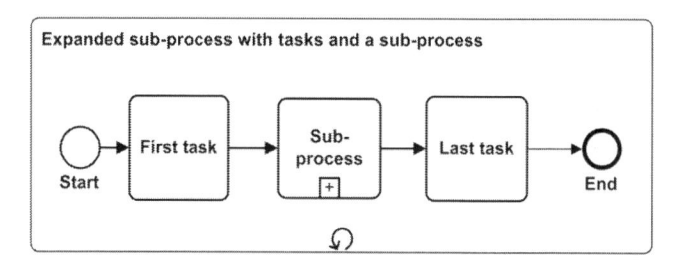

Expanded sub-process with tasks and a sub-process

Start → First task → Sub-process [+] → Last task → End

In the above example, the *Expanded Sub-process* is a looping sub-process, depicted by the *Loop* symbol centre bottom. A collapsed sub-process has been included to show the use of a granulated process.

Task Types

There are different types of tasks identified within BPMN which represent different activities.

Abstract Task

An *Abstract Task* is shown by a rectangle with rounded corners. As there is no symbol, it is considered unspecified.

A task which is not specified by a specific activity indicator is called an *Abstract or Unspecified Task*.

Send Task

A *Send Task* is shown by a rectangle with rounded corners containing a filled envelope marker in the upper left corner.

The *Send Task* is used to show that a message is to be sent to an external participant, relative to the process.

Once the message has been sent, the task is completed.

The actual participant, to whom the message is sent, can be identified by connecting the send task to a participant, using a message flow connector.

Receive Task

A *Receive Task* is shown by a rectangle with rounded corners containing an unfilled envelope marker in the upper left corner.

When the *Receive Task* is used to start a process, the process sequence is controlled by the receipt of a message.

The *Receive Task* starts the process if the process sequence does not have a start event and the *Receive Task* has no incoming sequence flow.

If the *Receive Task* has an incoming sequence flow, the task is not used to start the process.

If the *Receive Task* references a message, there can only be one data output.

If a data output is referenced, it must be equivalent to the message defined by the incoming associated message.

Send and Receive Task Example

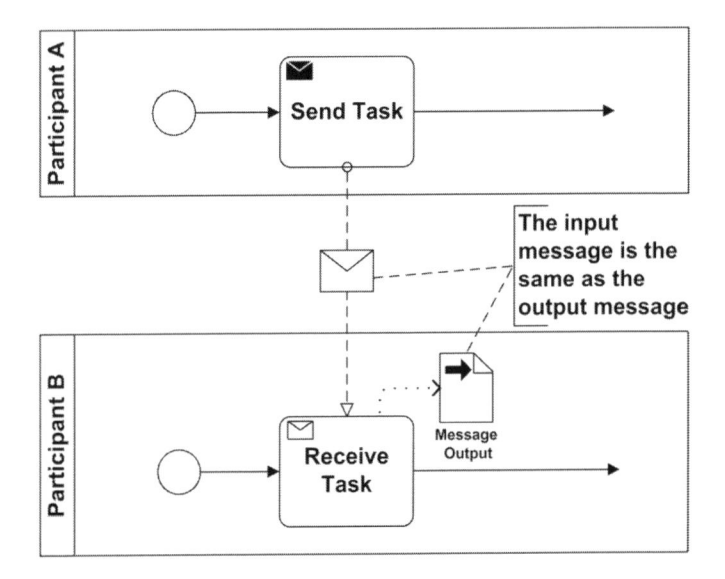

The above example shows two participants communicating.

Participant A sends a message from a *Send Task* and participant B receives the message with a *Receive Task*.

The message received by participant B is the output data object of the *Receive Task*.

Receive Task Initiating A Process

A *Receive Task Initiating A Process* is shown by a rectangle with rounded corners, containing a message start event notation in the upper left corner.

The *Receive Task Initiating A Process* does not require an incoming Sequence Flow and indicates that the process sequence will be started by a message received.

If the *Receive Task Initiating A Process* references a message, there can be one data output.

If a data output is referenced, it must be equivalent to the message defined by the incoming associated message.

One or more corresponding incoming Message Flows can be depicted on a BPD but the display of the message flows is not required.

Receive Task Initiating A Process Example

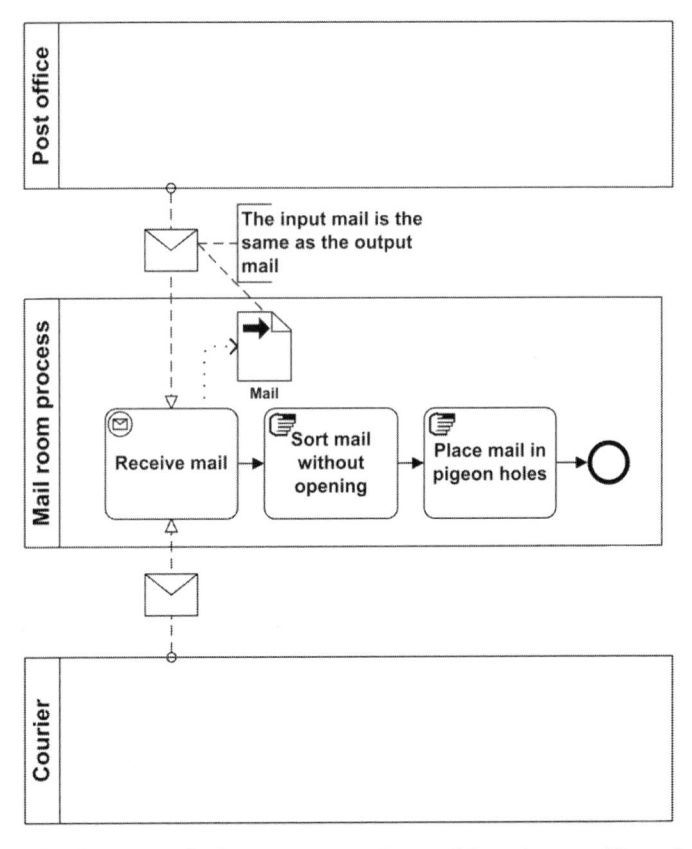

In the above example, the post room receives mail from the post office and different couriers.

When the mail is received the process to sort mail and place in pigeon holes is started by the *Receive Task Initiating A Process*.

Human Interactions Tasks

Human involvement is required to complete certain tasks specified in a workflow model.

BPMN specifies two different types of tasks with human involvement i.e. manual task and user task.

Manual Task

A *Manual Task* is shown by a rectangle with rounded corners with the addition of a hand figure marker, which distinguishes the shape as a manual task type.

The *Manual Task* is a task that is expected to be performed without the aid of any computer technology.

User Task

A *User Task* is shown by a rectangle with rounded corners with the addition of a human figure marker, which distinguishes the shape as a user task type.

The *User Task* is primarily used as a workflow task in which a human performs the task, with or without the assistance of a software application.

Business Rule Task

A Business Rule Task is shown by a rectangle with rounded corners with the addition of a chart shape in the upper left corner, indicating the task is a Business Rule Task.

The *Business Rule Task* provides a mechanism for the process to provide input to a business rules engine and to receive the output of calculations that the business rules engine provides.

The input output specification of the task allows the process to send data to and from a business rules engine.

Script Task

A *Script Task* is shown by a rectangle with rounded corners with the addition of a script shape in the upper left corner, indicating the task is a *Script Task*.

The *Script Task* activity is driven by a software application which executes the script. When the script is executed the task is complete.

Service Task

A *Service Task* is shown by a rectangle with rounded corners with the addition of a set of mechanical cogs in the upper left corner, indicating the task is a Service Task.

The *Service Task* links to an external service e.g. web application and has one input and at most one output. The *Service Task* is linked to a participant's service, using a message flow within a collaboration process.

Process Without Task Types Example

The following diagram depicts a process of selecting and booking a vacation. This example uses Abstract task elements.

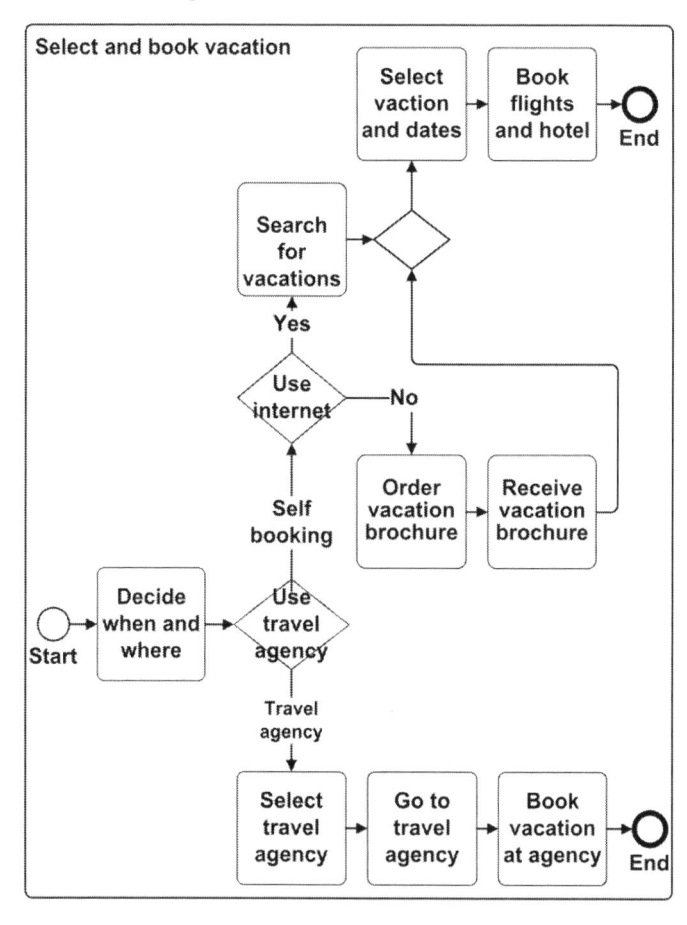

BPMN Pocket Reference

Using Task Types In A BPD

The previous process diagram can be described using task types instead of abstract tasks.

The following table describes the tasks used in the previous diagram and the associated task type.

Task	Type
Decide when and where	*User Task*
Use travel agency:	
• Select travel agency	*User Task*
• Go to travel to agency	*Manual Task*
• Book vacation at agency	*Service Task*
Self booking:	
• Use internet - Yes: Search for vacations	*Service Task*
• Use Internet - No: Order vacation brochure	*Send Task*
Receive vacation brochure	*Receive Task*
• Select vacation and dates	*User Task*
• Book flights and hotels	*Service Task*

Process With Task Types Example

Below depicts the previous BPD utilising the different task types.

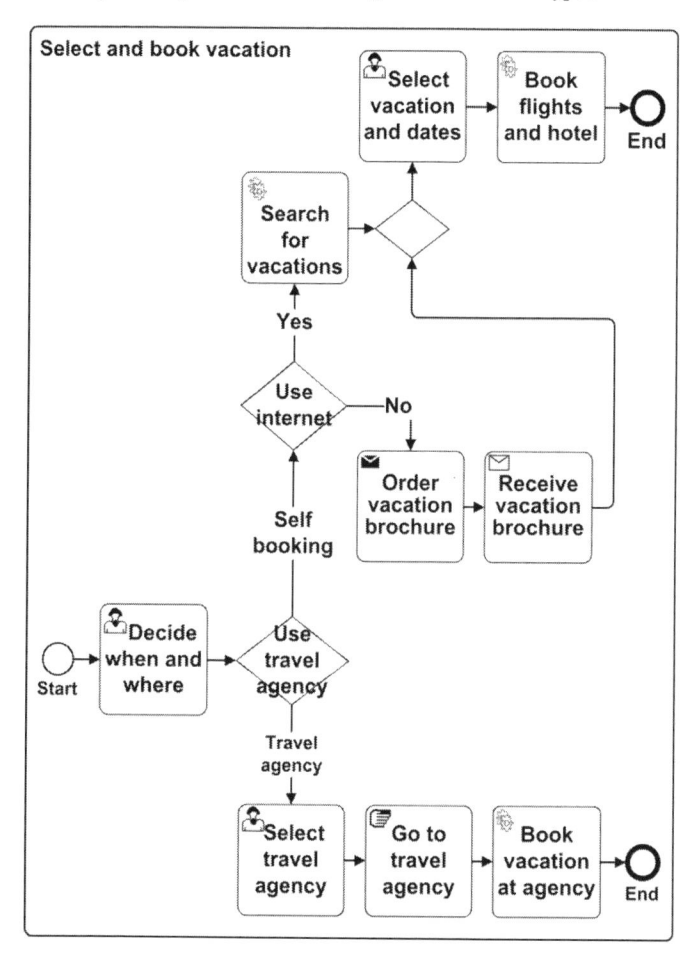

BPMN Pocket Reference

Call Activities

A *Call Activity* identifies a point in the process where a global process or a global task is used.

The activation of a *Call Activity* results in the transfer of control to the called global process or global task.

The *Call Activity* displays the marker of the type of global task (e.g., the call activity would display the *User Task* marker if calling a global user task).

If the details of the called process are available, then the shape of the *Call Activity* will be the same as an expanded sub-process, but depicted with a thick line.

When calling a global task, the *Call Activity* may have compensation and/or loop characteristic markers at the bottom centre of the shape, depending on the requirement.

Call Activity

A *Call Activity* object is shown by a thick lined rectangle with rounded corners.

Manual Call Activity

A *Manual Call Activity* object shares the same shape as the task and collapsed sub-process, with a thick line containing a hand figure marker that distinguishes the shape as a manual task type.

User Call Activity

A User Call Activity is shown by a thick lined rectangle with rounded corners, containing a human figure marker.

Business Call Activity

A *Business Call Activity* is shown by a thick lined rectangle with rounded corners, containing a chart shape in the upper left corner.

Script Call Activity

A *Script Call Activity* is shown by a thick lined rectangle with rounded corners, containing a script shape in the upper left corner.

Call Activity Calling A Process

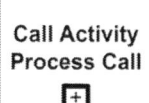

If details of a called process can be hidden, the shape of the call activity is shown by a thick lined rectangle with rounded corners, containing a plus sign.

Call Activity Expanded

If the details of the called process are available, then the shape of the *Call Activity Expanded* will be the same as an expanded sub-process, drawn with a thick line.

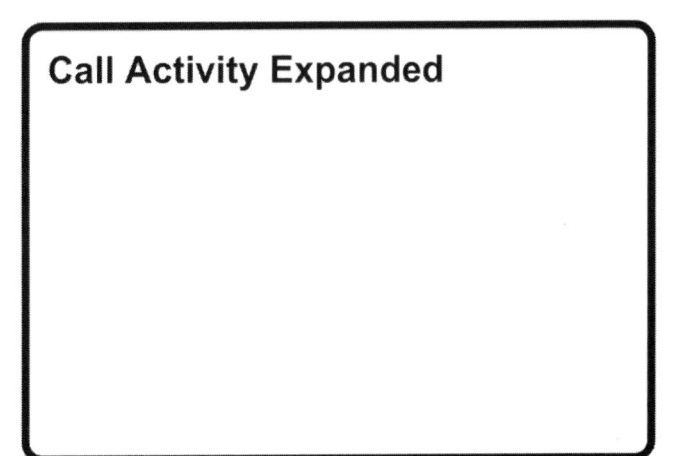

Call Activity Expanded

Connectors

Sequence Flows

———————Sequence Flow———————▶

A *Sequence Flow* is represented by a solid line with a solid arrowhead at one end.

Sequence Flows are used to show the order in which activities are executed within a process and used to connect tasks, sub-processes, events and gateways.

Conditional Flows

◇————Conditional Flow————▶

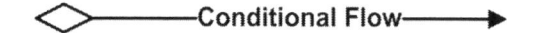

A *Conditional Flow* is depicted by a diamond shape at one end of the connector and a solid arrowhead on the other end.

Conditional Flows are used when specific conditions are met at a decision gate. The decision gate routes the direction of the process sequence flow.

Default Sequence Flows

⤼————Default Sequence Flow————▶

A *Default Sequence Flow* has a small cross line at one end of the connector and a solid arrowhead on the other end.

Default Sequence Flows are used when no other conditions are met.

Sequence flow Example

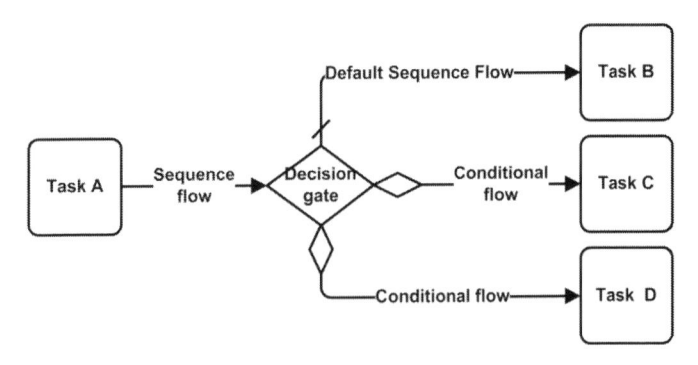

The above diagram shows three outputs coming from a decision gate.

Two of the outputs are conditional.

If the conditions are not met, the default connector automatically becomes the sequence flow.

Message Flows

o— — — — Message Flow — — —▷

A *Message Flow* is depicted by a dashed line with an open arrowhead at one end.

Message Flows are used to show the flow of messages between two separate process participants (business entities or business roles).

Message Flows allow modelling the order of tasks or sub-processes between organisations or departments which are in different pools.

Initiating Message Flows

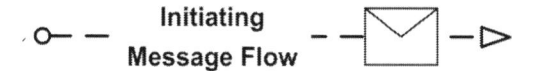

Initiating Message Flows are depicted by a dashed line with an open arrowhead at one end and an unfilled envelop denoting a starting message.

None Initiating Message Flows

None Initiating Message Flows are depicted by a dashed line with an open arrowhead at one end and a lightly filled envelope denoting a responding message.

Association

An *Association* is depicted by a dashed line.

Associations are used to connect information and artefacts with flow objects, such as tasks, sub-processes or events.

Directional Association

A *Directional Association* is depicted by a dashed line with a plain open arrow head at one end.

Bi-directional Association

← — — — _Bi- Directional _ _ _ →
             Association

A *Bi-directional Association* is depicted by a dashed line with a plain open arrow head at both ends.

Conversational link

═══════ Conversation ═══════
              Link

A *Conversational Link* is depicted by two thin parallel lines.

Conversational Links are used in conjunction with Conversation Nodes to describe a set of message flows between two participants in a collaboration process.

Two or more pools can use the conversation link with a conversation node to describe types of conversations.

Messages

A Message represents the content of a communication between two participant pools in a collaboration process.

In collaboration diagrams, a message flow symbol is included to show that a message is passed from one participant to another.

There are two message types:

Initiating Message

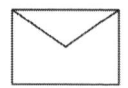

An *Initiating Message* is depicted by an unfilled envelope drawn with a single thin line.

Non-Initiating Message

A *Non-Initiating Message* has the same symbol as the *Initiating Message* but the envelope is shaded with a light fill.

Message Exchange Example

The following diagram describes the interaction using messages between two participating pools i.e. a customer and a supplier.

Message flows are only used between two external pools. The *Initiating Message* is sent by the customer pool and the responding *Non-Imitating Message* is sent by the supplier.

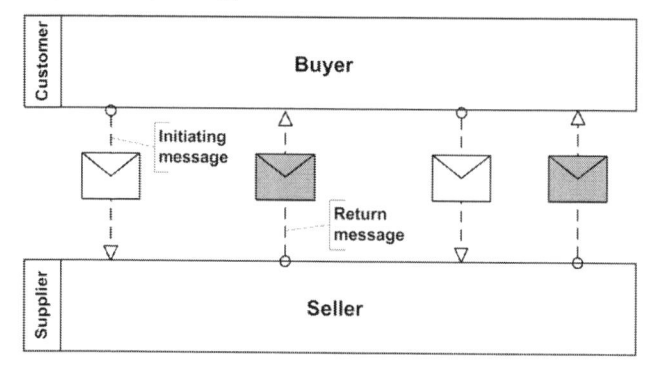

Messages With Choreography Tasks

In this example, the choreography is part of a collaboration process.

Message flows will pass-through a choreography task as they connect from one participant to another i.e. customer and supplier.

The buyer (customer pool) sends an order to the seller (supplier pool) with an *Initiating Message*.

The seller (supplier pool) confirms the order depicted by a *Non-Initiating Message*.

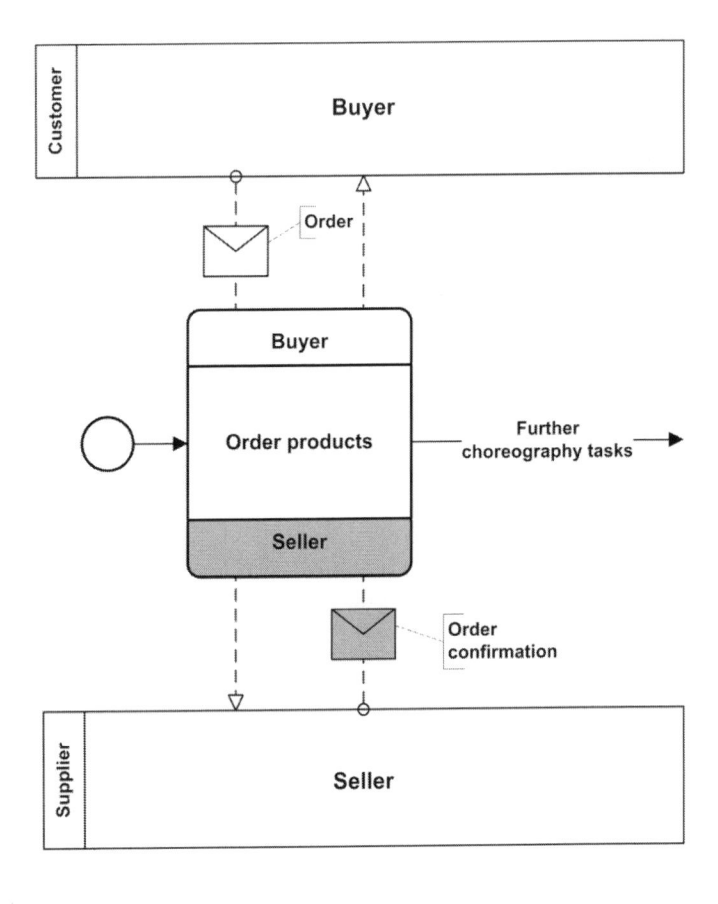

Conversations

Conversation Node

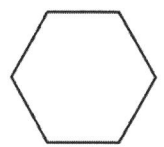

A *Conversation Node* is a hexagon drawn with a thin single line.

Conversation Nodes are used to represent a set of message exchanges.

Conversation Nodes represent message flows grouped together, based on a specific concept e.g. order, order confirmation and delivery note.

Conversation Nodes always involves two or more participant process pools.

Message Flow Example

The following diagram represents a simple collaboration message flow.

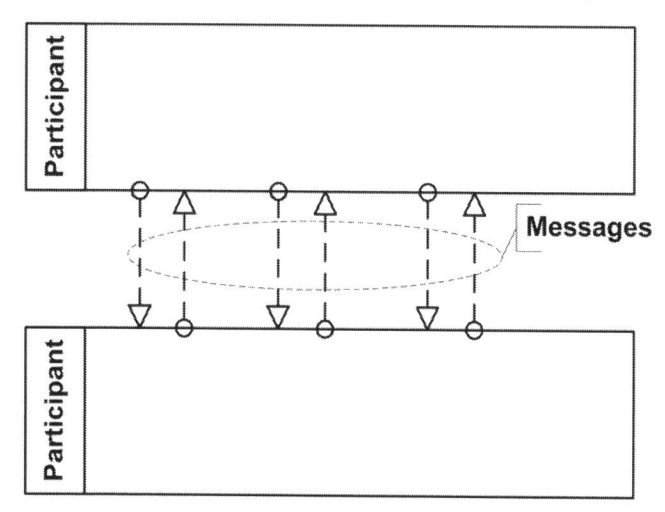

Conversation Node Example

The following diagram shows a *Conversation Node* depicting a message flow.

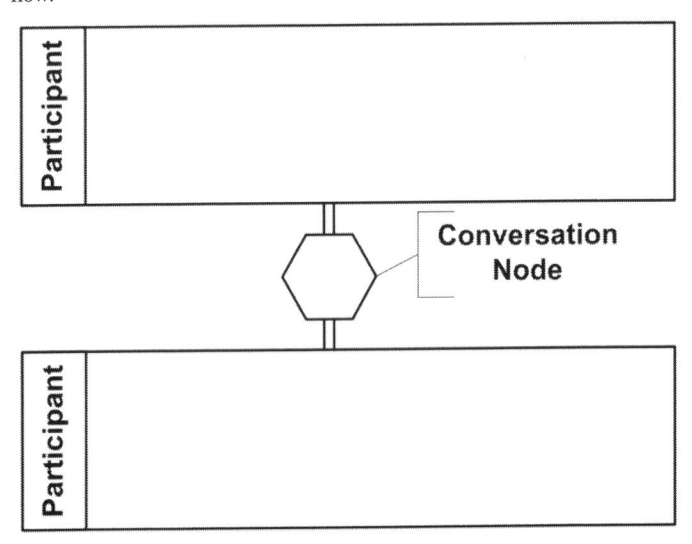

Conversation Node With Message Flows Example

The following diagram shows two pairs of message flows as well as a conversation node, between two participants.

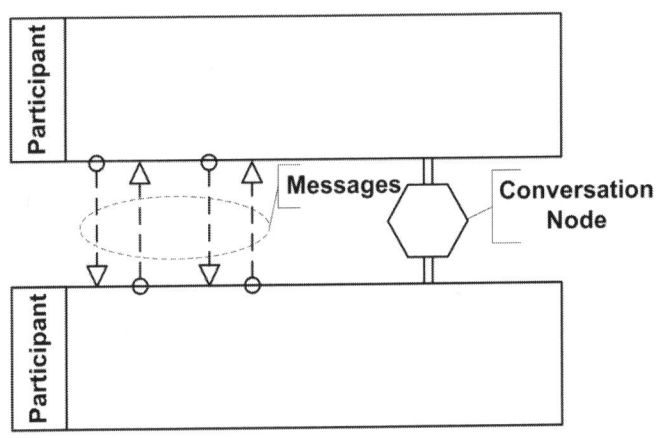

Sub-Conversation Node

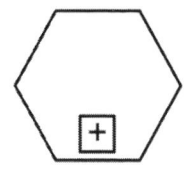

A *Sub-Conversation Node* is shown as a hexagon drawn with a thin line containing a square with a plus sign (+) bottom centre.

The *Sub-Conversation Node* is used within a collaboration process showing message flows, conversations and/or other *Sub-Conversations Nodes*.

Sub-Conversation Node Example

The following example shows the *Sub-Conversation* used to include different message flows and or conversations and if required, other *Sub-Conversation* nodes.

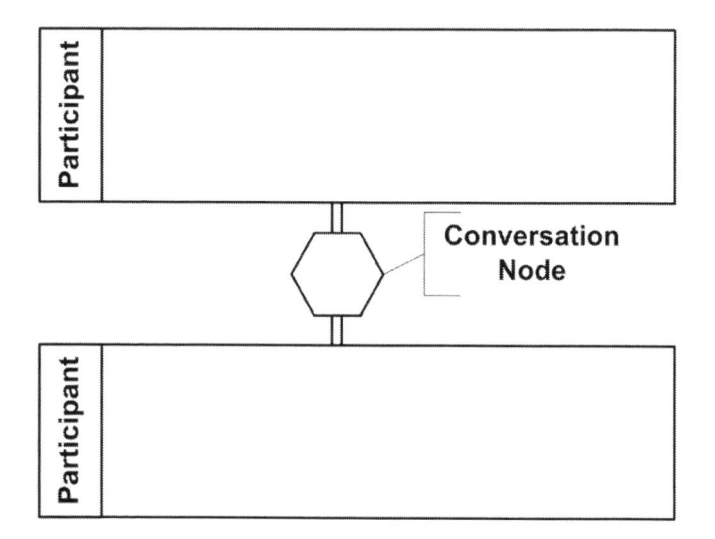

Global Call Conversation

A *Global Call Conversation* node is shown as a hexagon drawn with a thick line.

Global Call Conversations identify places in the conversation where a global conversation is required.

Collaboration Call Conversation

A *Collaboration Call Conversation* node is shown as a hexagon drawn with a thick line containing a small square with a plus sign (+) marker. The marker is positioned at the bottom centre.

Collaboration *Call Conversations* are used to call a collaboration process.

Choreography

Choreography is self-contained, it is not a pool or orchestration but a definition of the behaviour between interfacing participants.

Choreography defines the sequence of interactions between participants and only exists outside of or in between, process participant pools.

A choreography sequence involves two or more participants and each sequence is made up of choreography activates.

The status of the choreography is shown through the messages that are sent and received.

Choreography Tasks Elements

A choreography task is an activity in a choreography process. It represents an interaction, which is a coherent set of message exchanges, between two participants.

Any communication between the participants is shown as a message flow.

Choreography Task

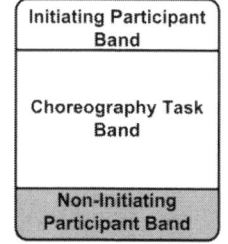

The *Choreography Task* is a rectangle divided into three bands that make up the shape's graphical notation.

The three bands are:

A. The *Initiating Participant Band* used for the Initiating Participants Name and is not shaded.

B. The *Choreography Task* Band is in the centre of the notation and used for the *Choreography Task* Name and is not shaded.

C. The *Non-Initiating Participant Band* used for the Non-Initiating Participants Name and is shaded.

The Initiating Participant Band can be either at the top or at the bottom.

The Non-Initiating Participant Band can be either at the bottom or at the top.

None Or Unspecified Choreography Task

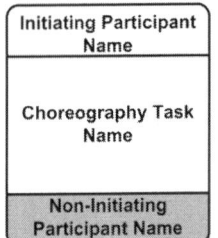

The *None Or Unspecified Choreography Task* is a rectangle depicted with three bands without distinguishable markers.

Choreography Task – Loop

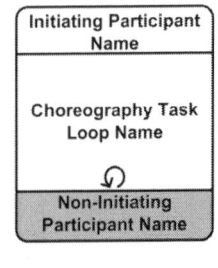

A *Choreography Task - Loop* is depicted as a rectangle with three bands containing with an arrow loop symbol at the centre bottom of the Choreography Task Band.

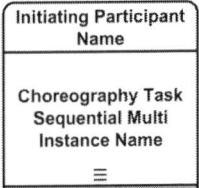

Choreography Task - Sequential Multi Instance

A *Choreography Task - Sequential Multi Instance* is depicted as a rectangle with three bands. The Choreography Task Band contains three parallel horizontal lines at centre bottom.

Choreography Task - Parallel Multi Instance

A *Choreography Task - Parallel Multi Instance* is depicted as a rectangle with three bands. The Choreography Task Band contains three parallel vertical lines at centre bottom.

Sub-Choreography Elements

A Sub-Choreography – Collapsed is a sub-process activity in a choreography process. It represents an interaction, which is a coherent set of message exchanges, between two participants.

The details of the *Sub-Choreography- Collapsed* are not visible in the diagram but the symbol indicates that the activity is a sub-process and has a lower level of detail.

Any communication between the participants is shown as a message flow.

Sub-Choreography - Collapsed

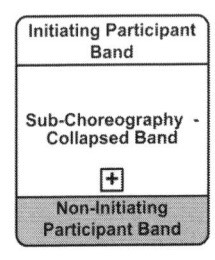

A *Sub-Choreography – Collapsed* is a rectangle divided into three bands that make up the shape's graphical notation. The Sub-*Choreography* Band contains a plus sign within a box at bottom centre.

The three bands are:

A. The *Initiating Participant Band* used for the Initiating Participants Name and is not shaded

B. The *Sub-Choreography – Collapsed Band* is in the centre of the notation and used for the Sub-*Choreography – Collapsed* Name and is not shaded

C. The *Non-Initiating Participant Band* used for the Non-Initiating Participants Name and is shaded

The Initiating Participant Band can be either at the top or at the bottom.

The Non-Initiating Participant Band can be either at the bottom or at the top.

None Or Unspecified Sub-Choreography - Collapsed

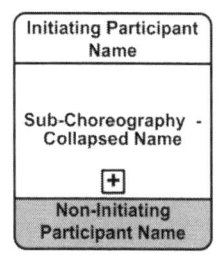

A None or Unspecified *Sub-Choreography – Collapsed* is a rectangle divided into three bands containing a plus sign at centre bottom of the Choreography Sub-process Band

Sub-Choreography Loop - Collapsed

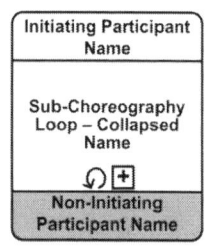

A *Sub-Choreography Loop – Collapsed* is depicted as a rectangle with three bands containing a loop symbol next to a plus sign within a box, at centre bottom of the Choreography Sub-process Band.

Sub-Choreography Sequential Multi-Instance – Collapsed

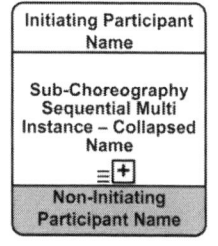

A *Sub-Choreography Sequential Multi Instance - Collapsed* is depicted as a rectangle with three bands containing a multi-instance symbol, three horizontal lines next to a plus sign within a box, at centre bottom of the Choreography Sub-process Band.

Sub-Choreography Parallel Multi Instance - Collapsed

A *Sub-Choreography Parallel Multi Instance - Collapsed* is depicted as a rectangle with three bands containing a multi-instance symbol, three vertical lines next to a plus sign within a box, at centre bottom of the Choreography Sub-process Band.

Choreography Sequence Flow

Sequence flows are used with choreographies to show the sequence of the choreography activities, which may also have intervening gateways to show forks, mergers and events.

Sequence Flows cannot cross the boundary of a Sub-Choreography and are only allowed to connect with other choreography activities.

Two Choreography Activities

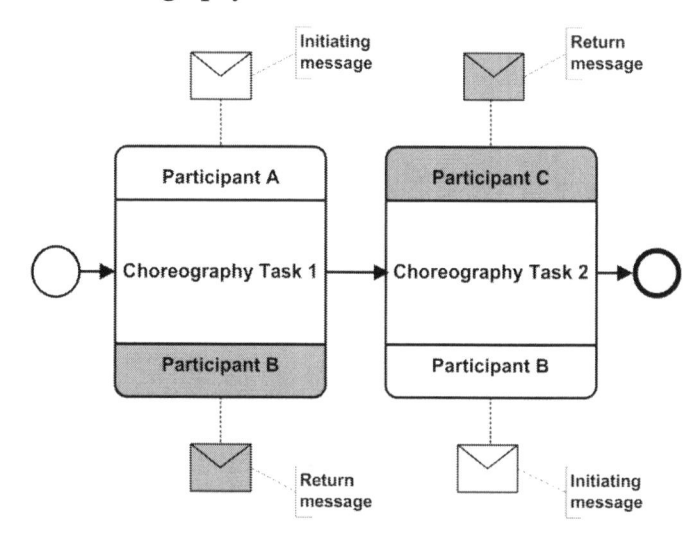

The above diagram shows a sequence of two choreography tasks with three participants.

Participant A sends a message and is the initiator of choreography Task 1.

Participant B responds with a message which may not be immediate since there can be internal work that the participant B needs to do prior to sending the return message.

Participant B sends the message and is the initiator of choreography Task 2.

Participant C does not know exactly when the message will arrive from participant B but is aware that one will arrive.

Participant C has no additional requirements until the message arrives.

Choreography Example

The following diagram shows a sequence of four choreography tasks with two participants i.e. Customer and Company.

1. Customer sends an order via email to Company
2. Company responds with a confirmation email
3. The product is delivered
4. Company sends an invoice
5. Customer sends a cheque

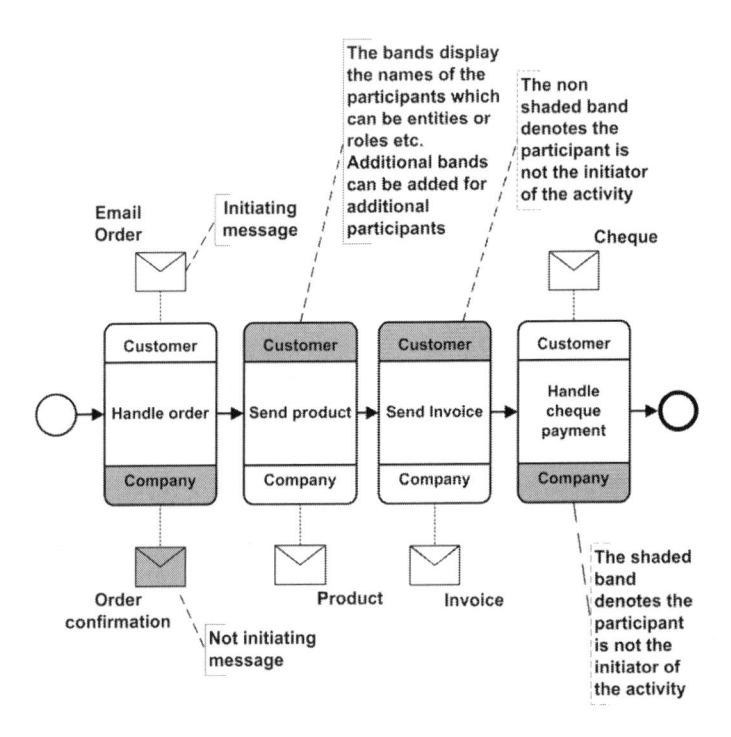

BPMN Pocket Reference

Choreography Within A Collaboration Example

1. The customer sends an order via email to a Computer Product Supplier.

2. The Computer Product Supplier responds with a confirmation email.

3. The sequence ends with the Computer Product Supplier sending an invoice.

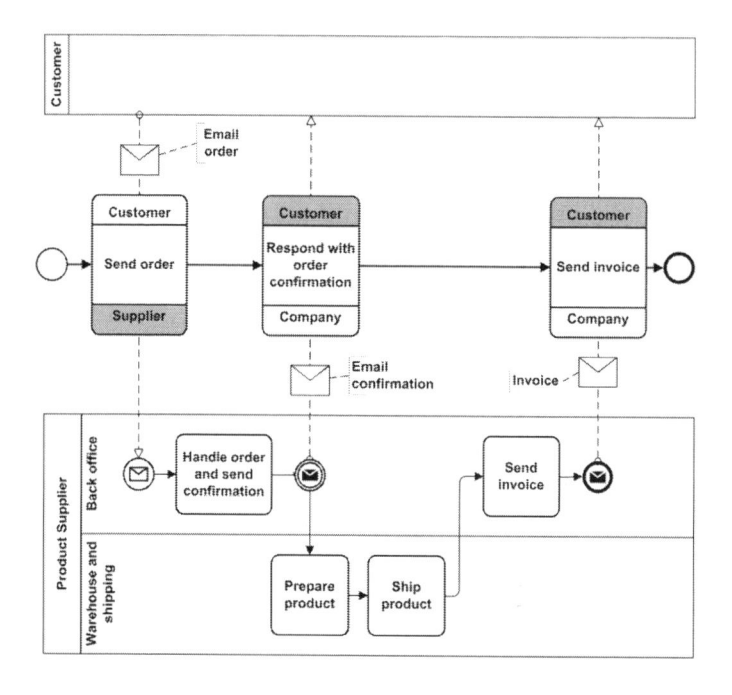

Artefacts

BPMN artefact elements

The current version of the BPMN specification pre-defines four types of *Artefacts*, Data Objects, Groups, Data Storage and Annotation.

Any number of *Artefacts* can be added to a diagram as appropriate for the context of the business processes being modelled.

Data Association

· · · ·Data Association· · · ·>

The *Data Association* is a dotted line with an open arrow.

The arrow should be used to describe the direction of the data object i.e. data creating the document or the document to be passed to another task or sub-process.

Data Objects

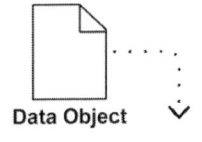

Data Objects are represented by a small rectangle with a turned over corner in the top right hand side.

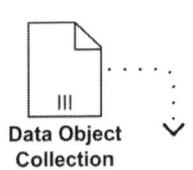

Data Object

Data Collection Objects are represented by a small rectangle with a turned over corner in the top right hand side with the addition of three lines on the bottom, depicting a collection of documents.

Data Object Collection

Data Objects are used to show how data is required or produced by activities.

The *Data Object* can be anything that is regarded as a data element i.e. letter, paper invoice, email, excel or word documents etc.

Data Input

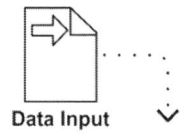

Data Input

Data Input elements are represented by a rectangle with a turned over corner in the top right hand side and a non filled arrow in the top left corner.

Data Input Collection

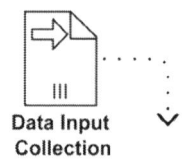

Data Input Collection elements are represented by a rectangle with a turned over corner in the top right hand side and a non filled arrow in the top left corner and three horizontal lines bottom centre.

Data Input elements provide information required by a task or sub-process.

The *Data Input Collection* describes a collection of documents.

The *Data Association* helps describe the direction of the data.

Data Output

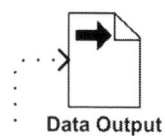

Data Output

Data Output elements are represented by a rectangle with a turned over corner in the top right hand side and a filled arrow in the top left corner.

Data Output Collection

Data Output Collection elements are represented by a rectangle with a turned over corner in the top right hand side and a filled arrow in the top left corner and three horizontal lines bottom centre.

Data Output elements provide information produced by tasks as an output, to be available for other tasks and sub-processes as an input.

The *Data Association* helps to describe the direction of the data.

Data Object Examples

The following example demonstrates using a *Data Object* as a single input and a *Data Object Collection* element.

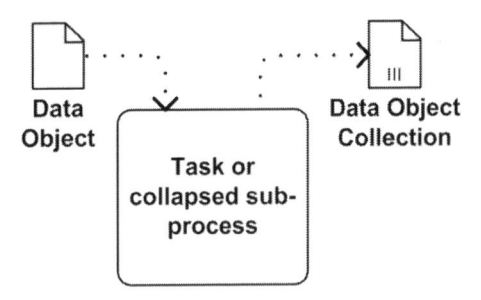

The following example demonstrates using a *Data Input* element and a *Data Output Collection* element.

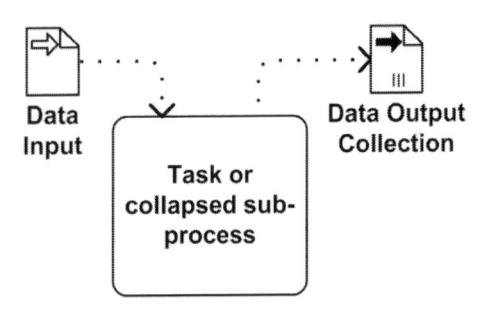

Group Notation

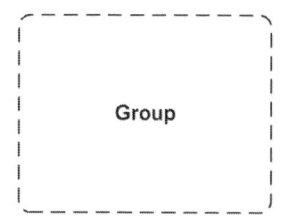

A *Group Notation* is represented by a rounded corner rectangle drawn with a dashed line.

Groups are used for documentation or analytic purposes, and do not affect sequence flows.

Groups are used to describe groups of tasks or sub-processes, which are part of the same operation, and are required to be performed in a specific manor.

Annotations

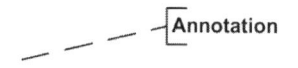

An *Annotation* is represented by a three sided partial box, containing the required description. The associated line is dashed without an arrow.

Annotations are mechanisms for modellers to provide additional text information for the reader of a Business Process Diagram.

Annotations are used to describe different parts of the diagram.

Data Store

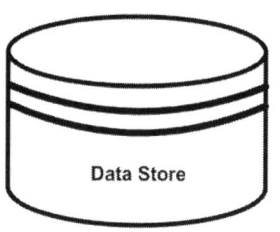

Data Store elements are depicted as a cylinder with two lines around the top.

A *Data Store* provides a source of data for activities to retrieve data or store data. A *Data Association* can be used to describe the direction of the data where required.

BPMN Pocket Reference

Gateways

Gateways are modelling elements used to describe how sequence flows merge, join or fork within a process.

Exclusive Gateways

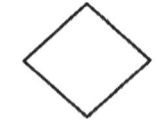

An *Exclusive Gateway* element is depicted by a diamond shape with or without an X.

The Exclusive Gateway is considered an *OR (XOR) and* has specific results, and instigates the way a process sequence flows.

Exclusive implies only one of many inputs or outputs are chosen from the gateway at any one time.

Exclusive OR Merge Example

In the following example, the three inputs merge together at the *Exclusive Gateway* which only allows one of the tasks A, B or C to continue to flow to task D at any one time.

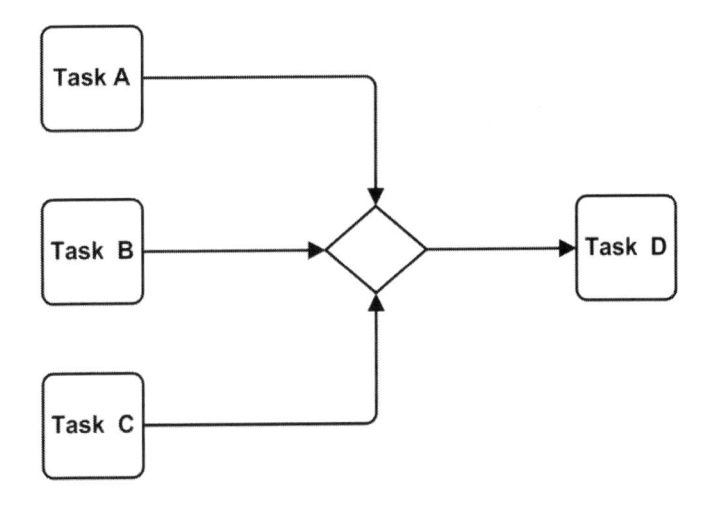

Data-Based XOR

A *Data-Based XOR* has the same effect on the sequence flow as the Exclusive OR Merge however, in reverse.

A *Data-Based XOR* is drawn with or without an X.

A *Data-Based XOR* controls the sequence flow coming into the gate and takes only one of the branches.

The expression at the gateway will decide which branch of the gateway is taken.

Data-Based XOR Example

In the following example, the Task A input splits at the *Data-Based XOR* into three branches.

The output path is chosen, depending on the conditions of each branch of the gateway.

The example shows three outputs

- Always Condition
- Alternative
- Default Alternative

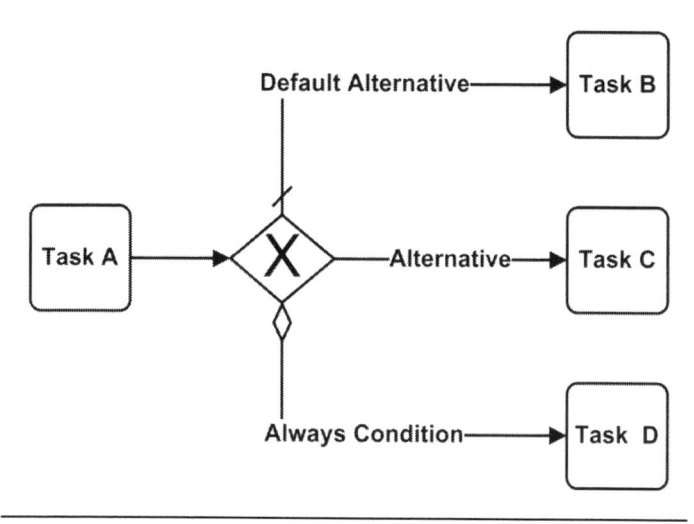

BPMN Pocket Reference 51

Exclusive Event-Based Gateways

An *Event-Based XOR Gateway* is shown as a diamond shape containing two thin circles surrounding a pentagon.

Event-Based XOR Gateways are used when multiple events merge or fork.

The output of the gateway will depend on the decision at the gateway.

Exclusive denotes that only one of many inputs or outputs is chosen to be the output from the gate, at any one time.

Merge Event-Based XOR Gateway

A Merge *Event-Based XOR Gateway* is used when only one output is permitted from multiple inputs.

Merge Event-Based XOR Gateway Example

In the following example, the three inputs merge together at the *Event-Based XOR Gateway*.

The gateway only allows one of the following inputs, Task A, Start Message event or Intermediate Timer event to continue the sequence flow to Task B at any one time.

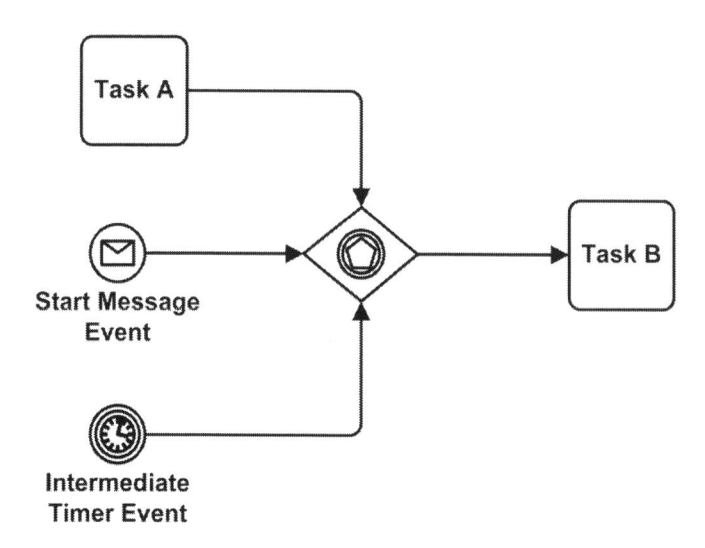

BPMN Pocket Reference

Fork Event-Based XOR Gateway

A *Fork Event-Based XOR Gateway* has the same effect as the *Merge Event-Based XOR Gateway* however, in reverse.

A *Fork Event-Based XOR Gateway* controls the sequence flow coming into the gate and can take only one of the outputs.

The expression at the gateway decides which branch of the gateway is taken.

Fork Event-Based XOR Gateway Example

In the following example, Task A output splits at the *Fork Event-Based XOR Gateway* into three branches Task B, End Message Event or Intermediate Timer Event.

The output path is chosen based on conditions at each branch of the gateway.

The example shows three outputs

- Task B
- End Message Event
- Intermediate Timer event

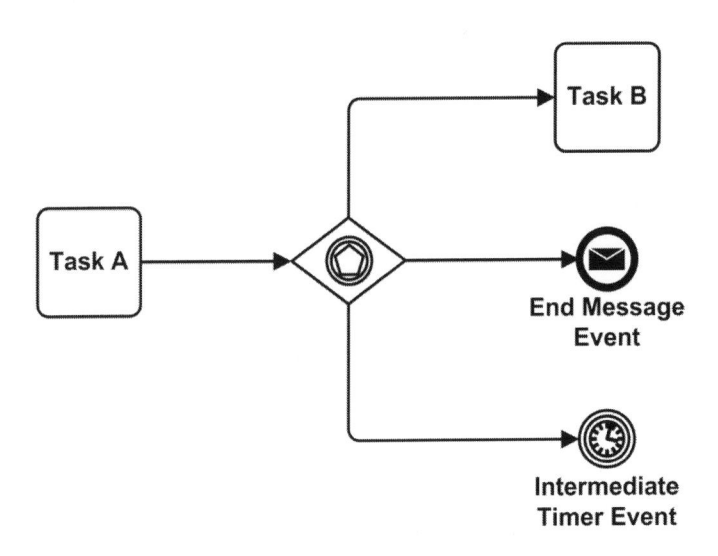

Parallel Gateways

A *Parallel Gateway* is shown as a diamond shape with a plus sign in the centre.

Parallel Forking Gateway Example

The *Parallel Forking Gateway* is also called an AND gateway. All sequence flows that branch out of the AND gateway are used.

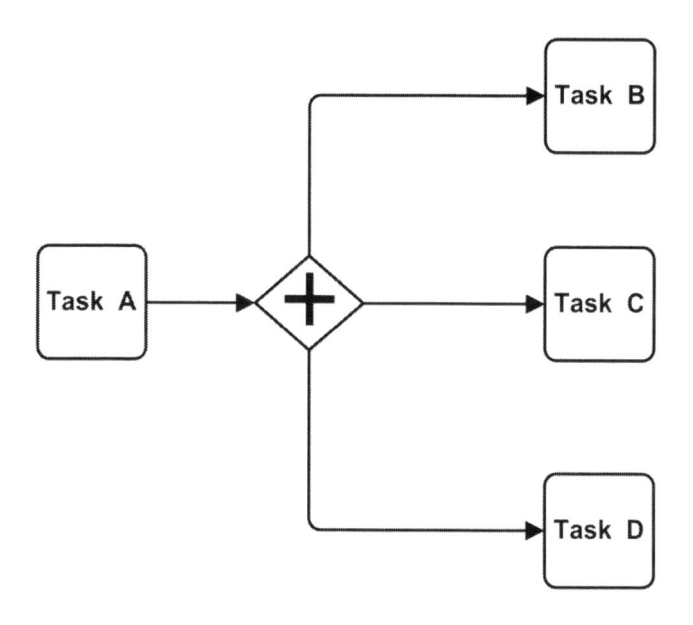

Parallel Joining Gateway Example

The *Parallel Joining Gateway* must receive an input from all input sequence flows, for the output flow to be used.

The process flow waits for all inputs to arrive at the AND gateway before continuing.

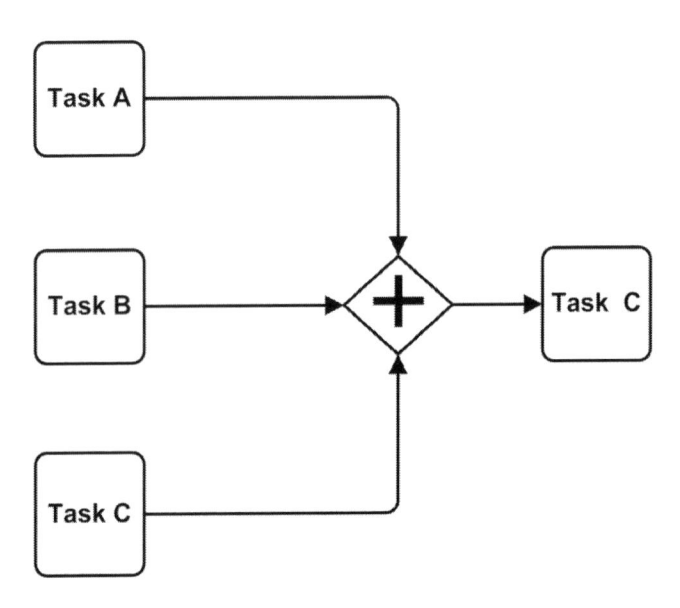

Inclusive Gateways

An *Inclusive Gateway is shown as* a diamond shape containing a circle.

Inclusive OR Decision Gateway Example

The *Inclusive OR Decision Gateway* allows the outgoing sequence flows from the gateway to be used depending on the condition.

When no decision is made by the gate the output will take the default sequence flow.

The following example shows the sequence flow from Task A branching to Tasks B,C, D, depending on the gateway decision.

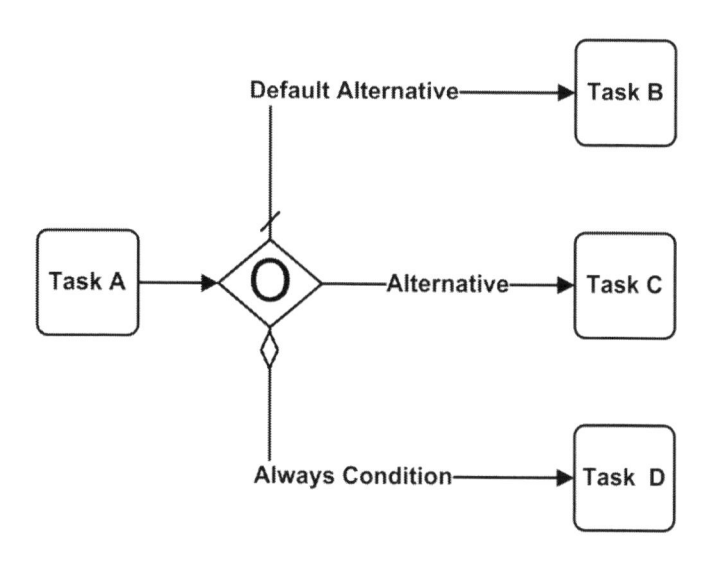

Inclusive OR Merge Gateway Example

The *Inclusive OR Merge Gateway* signifies that the process flow continues when the first input arrives from any of the input Sequence Flows.

If other inputs subsequently arrive from other input Sequence Flows, they are not used.

The following example shows the Sequence Flow from three different tasks merging into an *Inclusive OR Merge Gateway*.

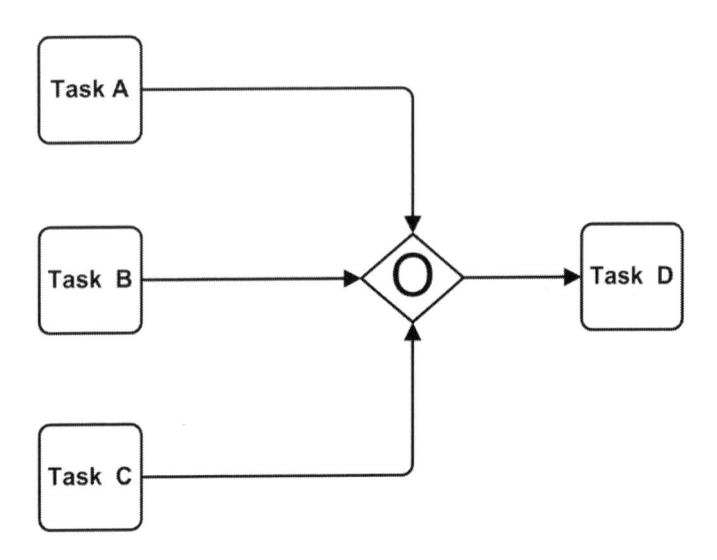

Complex Gateways

A *Complex Gateway* is shown as a diamond shape containing a merged plus and cross symbol.

Complex Decision Gateways

A *Complex Decision Gateway is* a specific complex flow condition, which references outgoing sequence flow names..

Complex Decisions Gateway Example

The *Complex Decision* Gateway determines which output flow is to be taken.

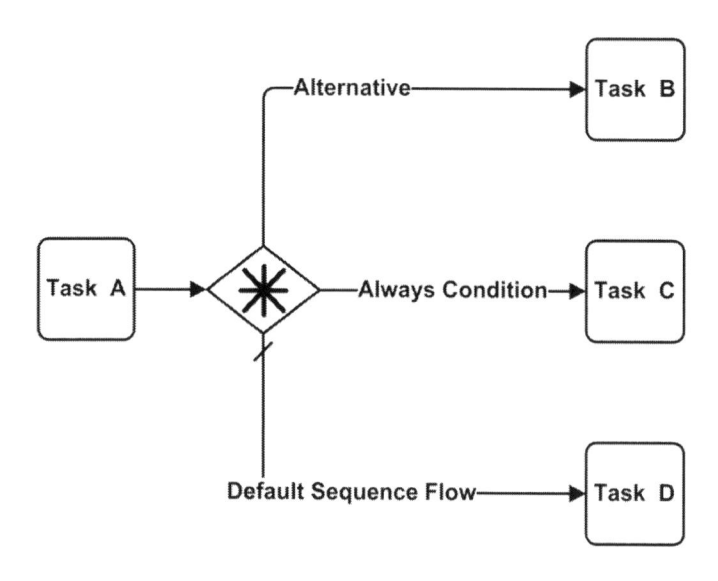

Complex Merge Gateways

A Complex Merge Gateway is a specific complex flow condition, which references incoming sequence flow names and/or process data that is merging into the gateway.

Complex Merge Gateway Example

The *Complex Gateway Merge* determines which one of the inputs from Task A, Task B or Task C flows to Task D.

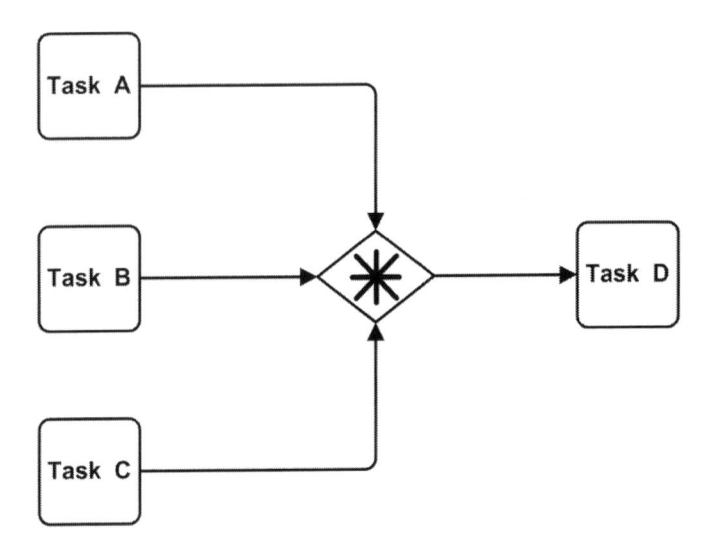

Process Pools and Swimlanes

Process Pool

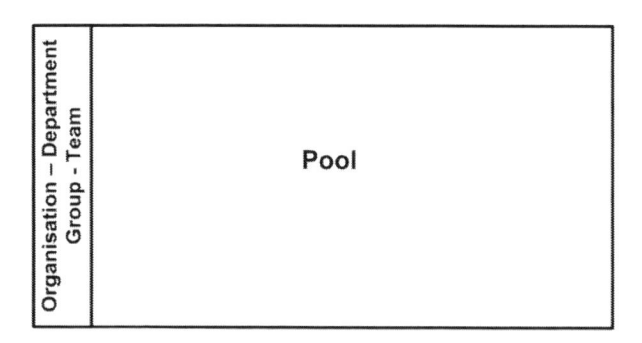

```
Organisation – Department
Group - Team             |          Pool
```

A *Pool* is represented by a rectangle, either horizontally or vertically.

A *Pool* name is on the left side for a horizontally pool and on top for a vertical pool.

A *Pool* acts as a container for a process, representing a participant in a business process diagram.

A *Pool* represents a process of an organisation e.g. company, department, group or team.

A *Pool* acts as a graphical container for partitioning a set of activities.

A *Pool* is an internal process which generally focuses on a single business organisation, and is considered a self-contained process.

Multi Instance Pool

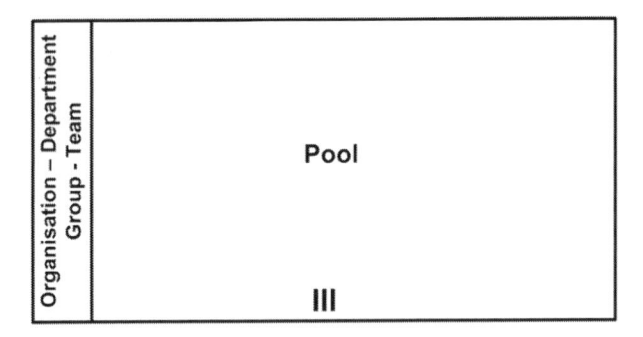

A *Multi Instance Pool* is represented by a rectangle either horizontally or vertically, containing three parallel vertical lines in the bottom centre.

A *Multi Instance Pool* is used when two or more of the same pool processes are performed simultaneously.

Swimlanes

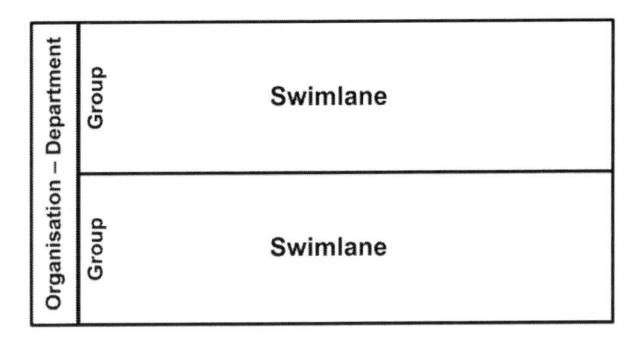

Swimlanes are sub-partitions within a pool and extend the entire length of the pool, either vertically or horizontally, the same as the parent pool.

Swimlanes are used to organise and categorise activities of departments, groups or teams etc. which make up the total process within the pool.

Communication Between Pools

Message flows are used to show the flow of messages between two or more pools.

Message flows connect either to the pool boundary or directly to flow objects within the pool boundary.

o— — — — Message Flow — — —▷

Message flows cannot connect two objects within the same pool or within swimlanes.

————————Sequence Flow————————▶

Sequence flows are used to connect flow objects within pools and swimlanes.

Pools And Swimlanes Example

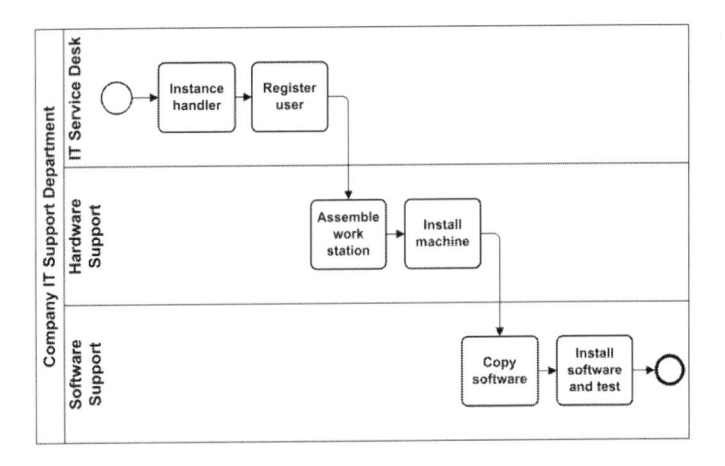

The above example demonstrates a process sequence flow and the interaction between the swimlanes.

In this example, the Company IT Support organisation is the process pool and each of the three following groups are shown in separate swimlanes.

- IT Service Desk
- Hardware Support
- Software Support

Black And White Box Pools

A *White Box Pool* shows a process sequence with activities and events required by the process.

A *Black Box Pool* does not show any activities and is an unknown process.

Black And White Box Pools Example

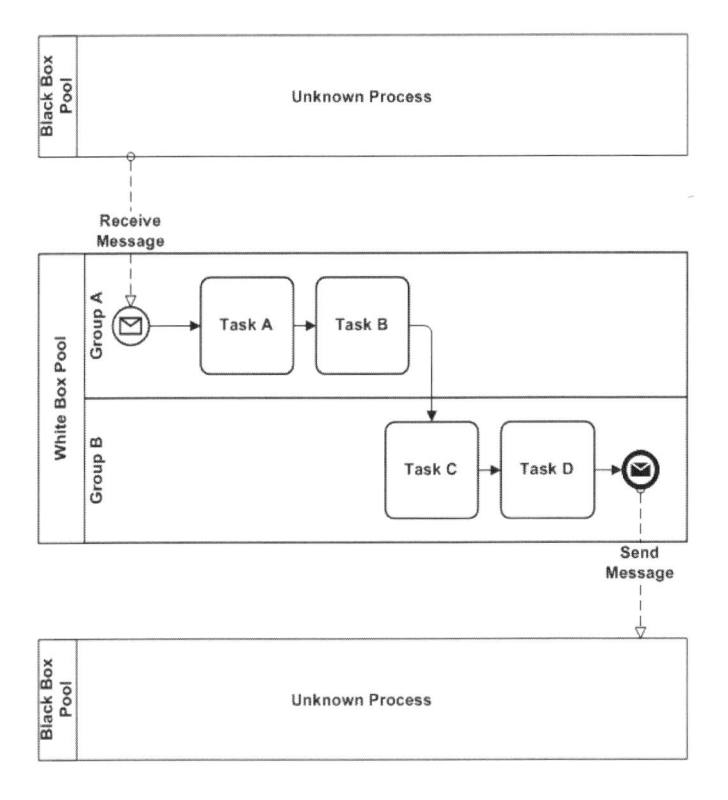

The above example demonstrates the communication between one *White Box Pool* and two *Back Box Pools*.

One *Black Box Pool* sends a message to start the *White Box Pool* process sequence.

The *White Box Pool* process sequence ends with an event sending a message to the other *Black Box Pool*.

BPMN Pocket Reference

Start Events

A *Start Event* triggers a business process or sub-process.

Interrupt And Non-interrupt Start Events

A start event is used to start a top level process sequence, an interrupting sub-process or non-interrupting sub-process.

The sub-process start event interrupts the sequence flow and returns when the sub-process has been completed.

If the sub-process start event is a non-interrupting start event, the top level sequence flow continues while the sub-process proceeds, thus not interrupting the top level sequence.

None Or Unspecified Start Event

A *None or Unspecified Start Event* is drawn as a thin line circle.

When a process does not need a start trigger, a *None or Unspecified Start Event* is used.

The *None or Unspecified Start Event* can be used to start a sub-process but cannot be used to start a non interrupt sub-process.

None Or Unspecified Start Event Example

In the following example, the start event is unknown therefore the *None or Unspecified Start Event* is used.

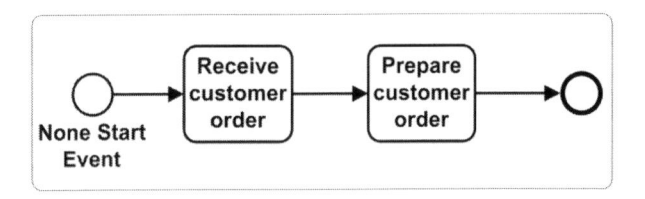

Message Start Event

A *Message Start Event* is a catching event and is depicted by a circle containing an unfilled envelope.

A *Message Start Event* used as a *Non-interrupt Event* is depicted with a dashed circle containing an unfilled envelope.

The *Message Start Event when* used in a sub-process can be an interruptible or a non-interruptible event.

The *Message Start Event* is used to begin a process when triggered by an outside process sending a message in a message sequence.

Message Start Event Example

In the following example, the process is started by an order coming from a customer, which can be an email or post.

This process is started by an external process pool.

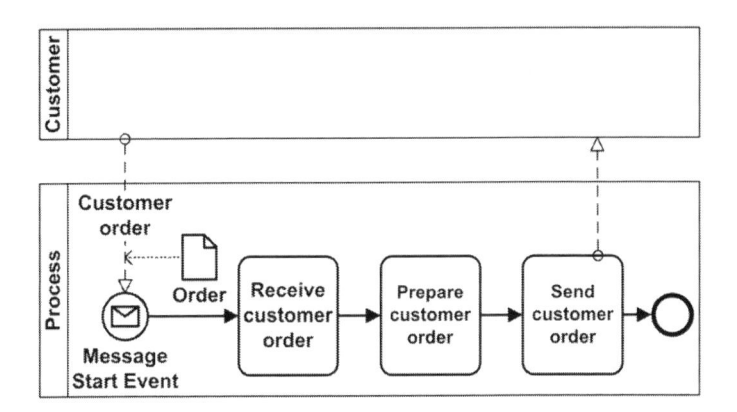

Timer Start Event

A Timer Start Event is a catching event and is depicted by a circle containing a clock face.

A *Timer Start Event* used as a *Non-interrupt Event* is depicted with a dashed circle containing a clock face.

The *Timer Start Event when* used in a sub-process can be an interruptible or a non-interruptible event.

The *Timer Start Event* is used to start a process at a specific time/date.

Timer Start Event Example

The following example shows the *Timer Start Event* triggering the process of checking customer orders from 10:00 which takes into account the post delivery.

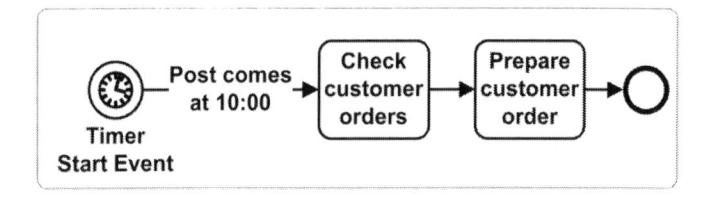

Conditional Start Event

A *Conditional Start Event* is a catching event and is depicted by a circle containing a rectangle with horizontal lines.

A *Conditional Start Event* used as a *Non-interrupt Event* is depicted with a dashed circle containing a rectangle with horizontal lines.

The *Conditional Start Event* when used in a sub-process can be an interruptible or non-interruptible event.

The *Conditional Start Event* is triggered when a specific condition occurs.

Conditional Start Event Example

The following example shows a *Conditional Start Event* triggering the bulk order process of 10 or more articles.

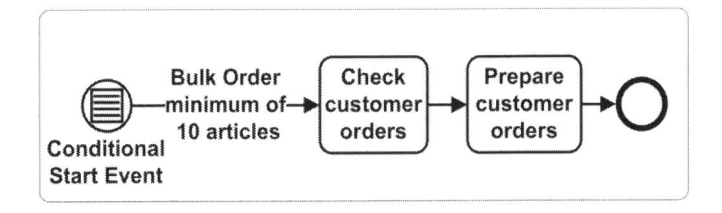

BPMN Pocket Reference   **69**

Multiple Start Event

A *Multiple Start Event* is a catching event and is depicted by a circle containing a pentagon.

A *Multiple Start Event* used as a *Non-interrupt Event* is depicted by a dashed circle containing a pentagon.

The *Multiple Start Event* when used in a sub-process can be an interruptible or a non-interruptible event.

The Multiple Start Event can be triggered by receiving any combination of a message start event, a timer start event, conditional start event or a signal start event.

The Multiple Start Event allows multiple methods of triggering the process however, only one of them is required to start the process.

Multiple Start Event Example

In the following example, the task 'Receive customer order' will be started, either by receiving the order by email or the morning post at 10:00.

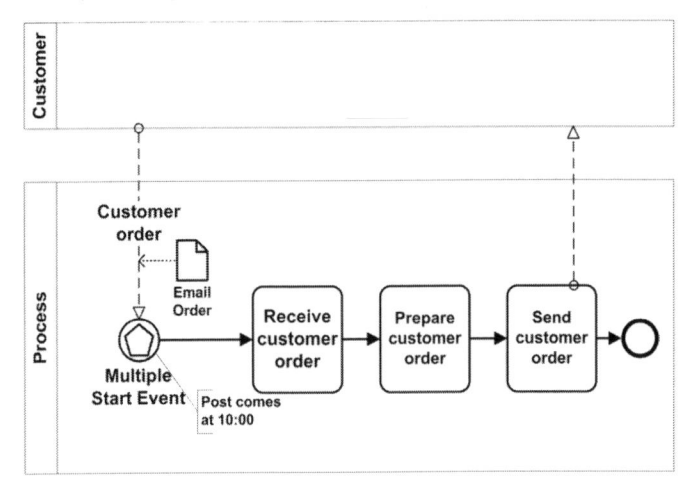

The above example shows the Multiply Start Event used for a Timer or Message event.

Parallel Multiple Start Event

A *Parallel Multiple Start Event* is a catching event and is depicted by a circle containing an unfilled plus sign.

A *Parallel Multiple Start Event* used as a *Non-interrupt Event* is depicted with a dashed circle containing an unfilled plus sign.

The *Parallel Multiple Start Event* when used in a sub-process can be an interruptible or a non-interruptible event.

The *Parallel Multiple Start Event* is triggered when two or more different types of start events occur at the same time.

This is in contrast to the *Multiple Start Event* where any of the assigned triggers can start the process.

Parallel Multiple Start Event Example

In the following example, the task 'Receive customer order' will only start after 09:00 even though an order could arrive much earlier.

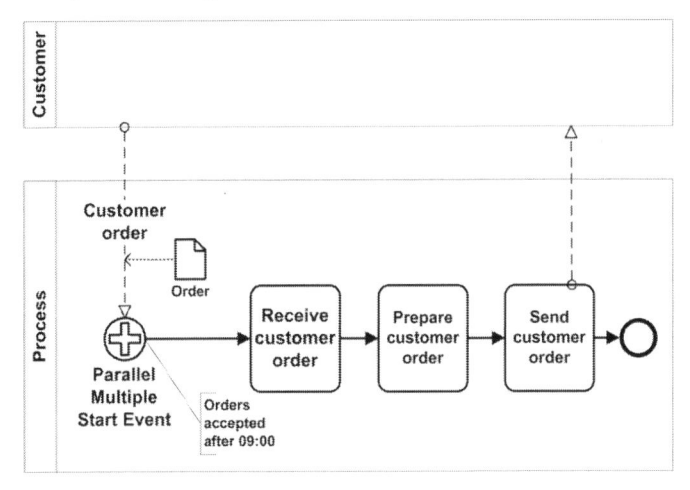

The above example shows the Parallel Multiply Start Event used for a Timer AND Message event.

BPMN Pocket Reference 71

End Events

When using BPMN to model business processes an *End Event* is required for the completion of any business process sequence.

None or Unspecified End Event

A *None or Unspecified* End Event is a circle drawn with a thick line.

The *None or Unspecified End Event* is used to describe the completion of a business process sequence when there are no other requirements associated with the end event.

This event can be used to end a sub-process even though it is not the end of the inline process sequence.

None or Unspecified End Event Example

In the following example, the process starts with a None Start Event and ends with a None End Event.

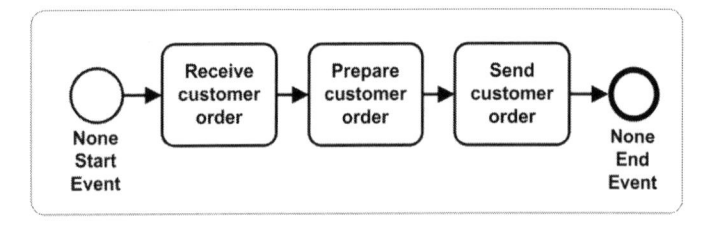

Message End Event

A *Message End Event* is a throwing event and is depicted by a circle containing a filled envelope.

The *Message End Event* is used to send a message to another process sequence via a message flow.

Message End Event Example

The following example shows the process beginning with a message start event triggered by receiving an order from a customer.

The customer order is processed and the process sequence is completed with a *Message End Event*, which shows an invoice being sent to the customer.

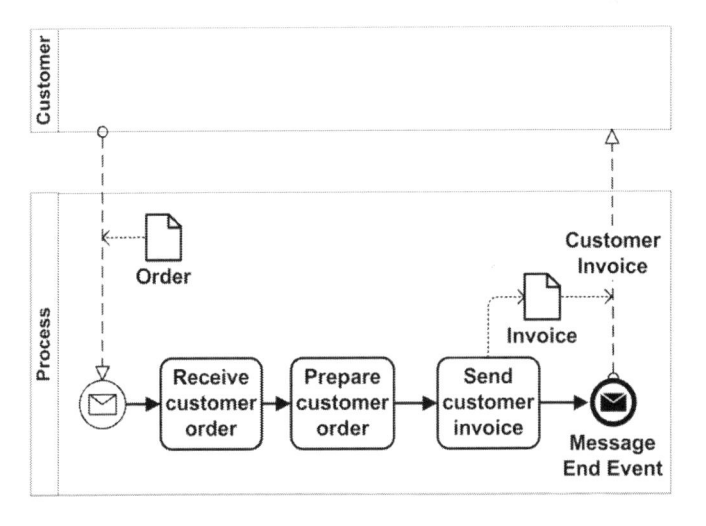

Multiple End Event

A *Multiple End Event* is a throwing event and is depicted by a circle containing a filled pentagon.

The *Multiple End Event* provides a way to simplify diagrams when specifying that more than one type of end event occurs at the completion of a process.

Multiple End Event Example

In the following example, the process begins with a message start event triggered by receiving an order from a customer.

The customer order is processed and the process sequence is completed with a *Multiple End Event*, which shows not only an invoice being sent to the customer but also the product.

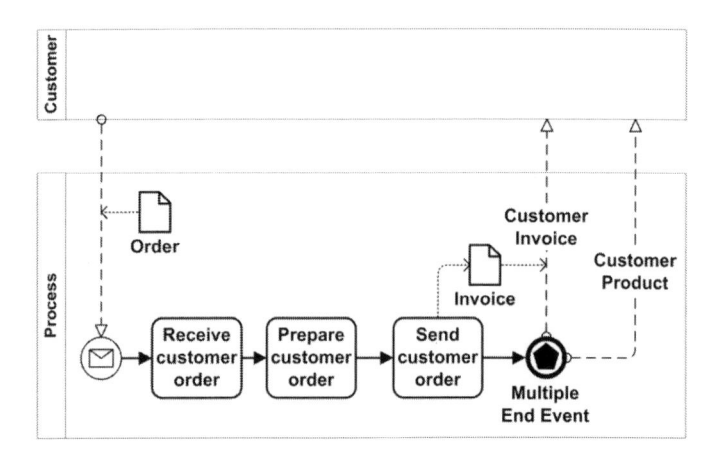

Terminate End Event

A *Terminate End Event* is depicted by a circle containing a large filled dot.

A *Terminate End Event* used in BPMN signifies that all activities in the process cease immediately.

When this event is used in a sub-process, the whole inline process stops and does not continue with any other tasks or sub-processes.

Terminate End Event Example

In the following example, the process begins with a message start event triggered by receiving an order from a customer.

The customer credit is checked and if not credit worthy the sub-process and the inline process is terminated immediately.

If the customer is credit worthy, the order is processed and the product and invoice are sent to the customer.

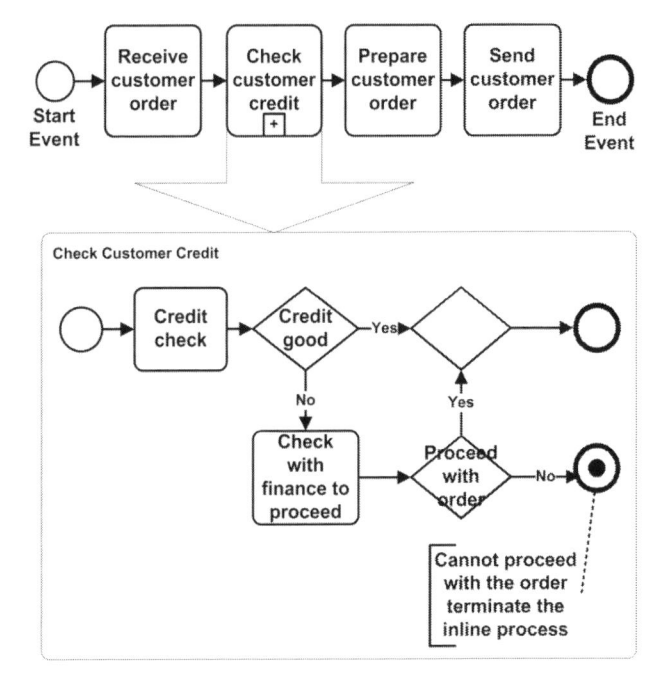

BPMN Pocket Reference 75

Inline Intermediate Events

An Intermediate Event is used to show where an event takes place in the sequence flow and is only used between the Start and End event.

Intermediate Events can affect the flow of the process sequence under certain conditions.

Intermediate Events can be used to

- show where messages are expected or sent within the process sequence
- show where delays are expected within the process sequence
- show where the sequence flow is controlled under certain conditions
- show where the sequence flow is interrupted and triggered by another event to continue
- show where the sequence flow of another process can be started or continued

None Or Unspecified Intermediate Event

A *None or Unspecified Intermediate Event* is depicted by two circles one drawn inside the other with a thin line.

An *Unspecified Intermediate Event* does not have a specific purpose but can be used in a variety of ways to detail a diagram.

An *Unspecified Intermediate Event* is only used within the process sequence flow.

None Or Unspecified Intermediate Event Example

In the following example, invoices are checked and are sent to the customer.

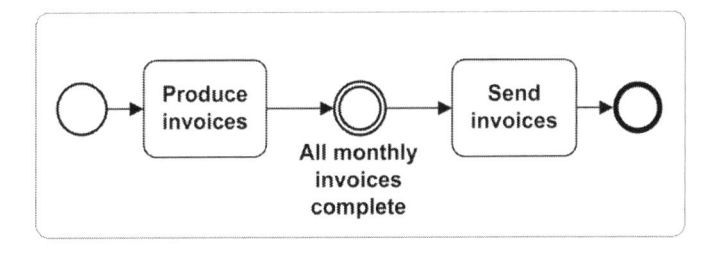

The *Unspecified Intermediate Event* shows that at this point in the sequence flow, the invoices are all completed.

Message Intermediate Catching Event

A *Message Intermediate Catching Event* is depicted by two circles drawn one inside the other with a thin line, containing an unfilled envelope.

The *Message Intermediate Catching Event* is used to stop the sequence flow until a message is received via a message flow connector, before continuing with the sequence flow.

Message Intermediate Throwing Event

A *Message Intermediate Throwing Event* is depicted by two circles drawn one inside the other with a thin line, containing a filled envelope.

The *Message Intermediate Throwing Event* is used in a sequence flow and does not change or stop the flow but causes a message to be sent to another process via a message flow connector.

Message Intermediate Event Example

In the following example, an order is received from a customer.

If parts are unavailable, an order is sent to a parts supplier, shown by a throwing event.

The sequence stops at the catching event waiting for a message before continuing.

The process sequence flow is triggered when parts are received from the parts supplier, shown by the catching event.

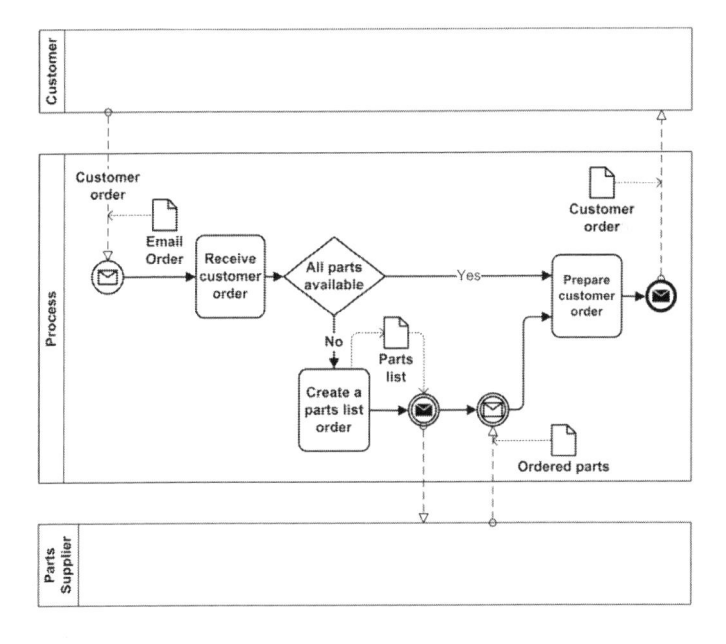

Timer Intermediate Catching Event

A *Timer Intermediate Catching Event* is depicted by two circles drawn one inside the other with a thin line, containing a clock face.

By using a *Timer Intermediate Catching Event* the sequence flow is stopped until either a time, a date, or a recurring time or date, allows the continuation of the process sequence flow.

Timer Intermediate Catching Event Example

In the following example, invoices are produced but the *Timer Intermediate Catching Event* only allows the sequence to continue at 16:00 when the post arrives.

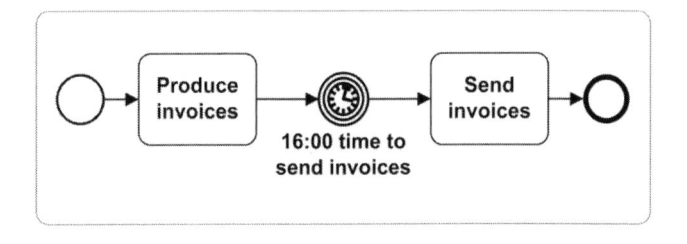

Conditional Intermediate Catching Event

A *Conditional Intermediate Catching Event* is depicted by two circles drawn with a thin line, containing a rectangle with horizontal lines.

A *Conditional Intermediate Catching Event* is triggered when a specific condition becomes valid.

The evaluation of the condition, initiates the continuation of the process sequence.

Conditional Intermediate Catching Event Example

In the following example, the invoices are checked and paid if they are due.

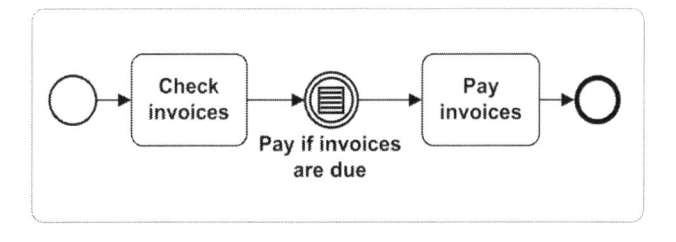

Multiple Intermediate Catching Event

A *Multiple Intermediate Catching Event* is depicted by two circles one drawn inside the other with a thin line, containing an unfilled pentagon.

The *Multiple Intermediate Catching Event* is used when more than one type of event occurs during the sequence flow.

The *Multiple Intermediate Catching Event* waits for any of the designated triggers before the sequence flow continues.

Any intermediate inline catching event can be included as part of the *Multiple Intermediate Catching Event*.

Multiple Intermediate Catching Event Example

In the following example, invoices are checked and paid if due or it is the end of the month.

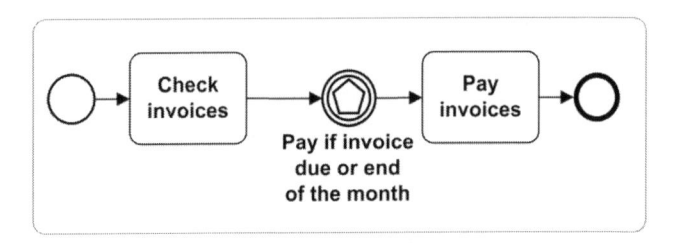

The Example *Multiple Intermediate Catching Event* is a Conditional **OR** Timer event.

Multiple Intermediate Throwing Event

A *Multiple Intermediate Throwing Event* is depicted by two circles one drawn inside the other with a thin line, containing a filled pentagon.

When used in a sequence flow, the *Multiple Intermediate Throwing Event* does not change or stop the flow but causes a trigger to be sent to other processes.

The *Multiple Intermediate Throwing Event* will throw all events specified at the same time.

The *Multiple Intermediate Throwing Event* can only include

- Message event
- Compensation event
- Signal throwing event

Multiple Intermediate Throwing Event Example

In the following example, an order is received from a customer.

If parts are unavailable, an order is sent to a parts supplier at the same time as a signal is sent to purchasing to update record orders.

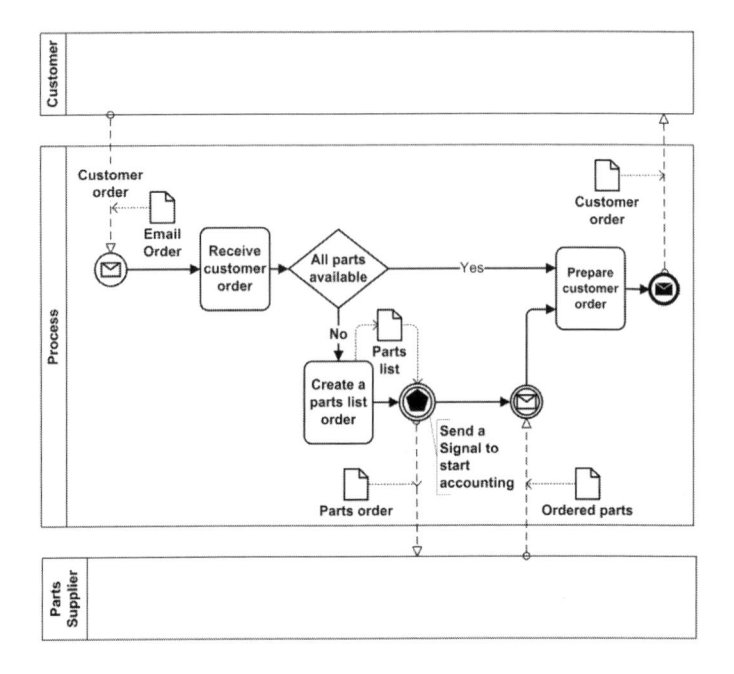

The example *Multiple Intermediate Throwing Event* is a combined Message and Signal event.

The *Signal Intermediate Throwing Event* triggers either a start or an intermediate catching signal event.

Parallel Multiple Intermediate Catching Event

A *Parallel Multiple Intermediate Catching Event* is depicted by two circles drawn one inside the other with a thin line, containing an unfilled plus sign.

The *Parallel Multiple Intermediate Event* is triggered when a group of several different events, each of which occur at the same time in order for the process flow to continue.

Any intermediate inline catching event can be included as part of the *Parallel Multiple Intermediate Event*.

Parallel Multiple Intermediate Catching Event Example

In the following example, invoices are checked and if due, and it is the end of the month, they are paid.

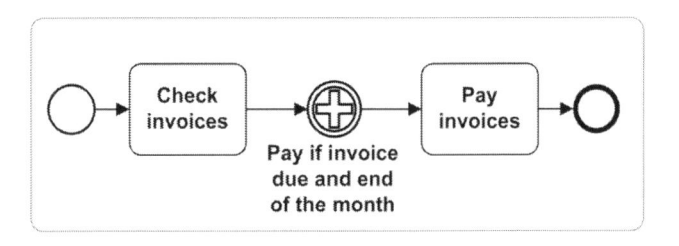

The example *Parallel Multiple Intermediate Catching Event* is a conditional **AND** timer event.

Intermediate Links

Intermediate links are a mechanism for connecting the end of one part of a sequence flow to another part of the sequence flow within a BPD.

Intermediate Links cannot be used to cross different BPDs.

*Intermediate Link*s are used in pairs i.e. a sequence end to a sequence start.

The *Intermediate Throwing Link* symbolises the start of the link.

An Intermediate Throwing Link is depicted by two circles one drawn inside the other with thin lines containing a filled arrow facing right.

The *Intermediate Catching Link* symbolises the end of the link and the continuation of the process sequence.

An Intermediate Catching Link is depicted by two circles one drawn inside the other with thin lines containing an unfilled arrow facing right.

Boundary Intermediate Events

An intermediate event is called a *Boundary Intermediate Event* when placed on the edge of a task or sub-process. It represents the deviation from the normal sequence flow of the process to an exception flow.

A *Boundary Intermediate Event* can be attached to any location on a task, a collapsed or an expanded sub-process boundary. The outgoing sequence can flow in any direction.

One or more *Boundary Intermediate Events* can be attached directly to the edge of a task or sub-process.

A *Boundary Intermediate Event* creates an exception flow, which may or may not reconnect with other tasks in the normal sequence flow.

A *Boundary Intermediate Event* cannot have an incoming sequence flow and as such, it can only be a source for a sequence flow.

Interrupt And Non-interrupt Boundary Intermediate Events

When the Boundary Intermediate Event interrupts the sequence flow of a task or a sub-process the normal sequence flow stops, while the exception flow is completed.

When the Boundary Intermediate Event is non-interrupting, the normal sequence flow continues in parallel with the exception sequence flow.

Message Intermediate Boundary Event

An interruptible *Message Intermediate Boundary Event* is depicted by two thin circles one drawn inside the other, containing an unfilled envelope.

A non-interruptible *Message Intermediate Boundary Event* is depicted by two thin dashed circles one drawn inside the other, containing an unfilled envelope.

The *Message Intermediate Boundary Event* is attached to the edge of a sub-process and when triggered changes the normal sequence flow into an exception sequence flow.

When the *Message Intermediate Boundary Event* is non-interrupting, the normal sequence flow continues in parallel with the exception sequence flow.

The actual participant, from which the message is received, is identified by connecting the sub-process to the participant using a message flow connector within a collaboration process.

Interruptible Message Intermediate Boundary Event Example

In this example, customers send orders which are handled by *Handle Orders* sub-process.

Each order will be processed and a work order produced.

If a customer needs to cancel their order, the *Handle Orders* sub-process is interrupted and the exception path continues to the *Cancel work order* task.

After the order has been cancelled the sequence returns to the normal sequence flow to *Update order records*.

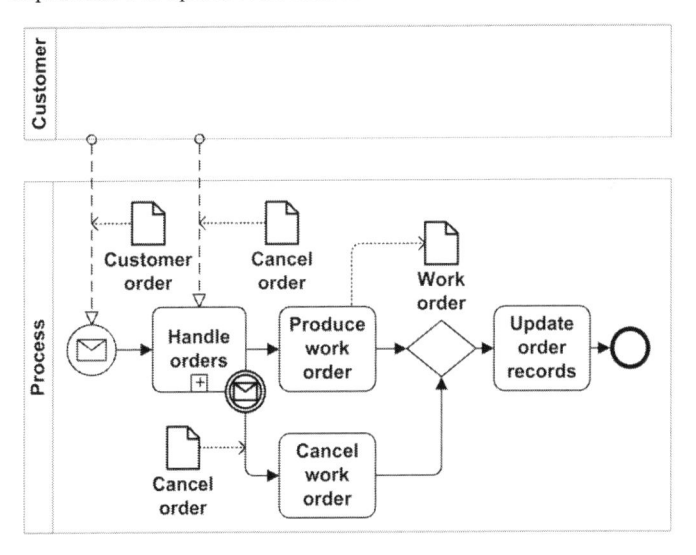

Non-Interruptible Message Intermediate Boundary Event Example

When the *Message Intermediate Boundary Event* is non-interrupting, the *Handle Orders* sub-process continues while the customer's order is updated.

In this example, customers send orders which are handled by *Handle Orders* sub-process.

Each order will be processed and a work order produced.

If a customer needs to change their order with a change order request, the *Handle Orders* sub-process will take an exception path to update the order.

As the *Message Intermediate Boundary Event* is non-interruptible the normal sequence will continue.

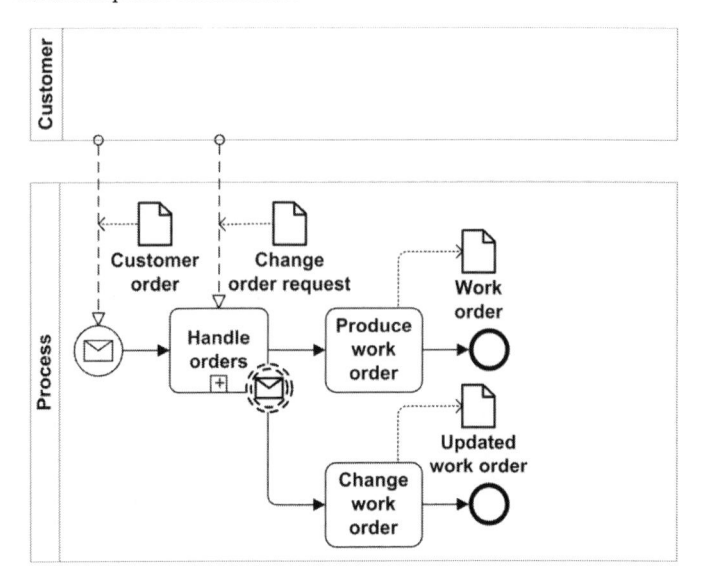

Timer Intermediate Boundary Event

An interruptible *Timer Intermediate Boundary Event* is depicted by two thin circles one drawn inside the other, containing a clock face.

A non-interruptible *Timer Intermediate Boundary Event* is depicted with two thin dashed circles one drawn inside the other, containing a clock face.

A *Timer Intermediate Boundary Event* is placed on the edge of a task or sub-process in order to interrupt the sequence flow at a set time or date during a task or sub-process activity.

The set time or date causes the task or sub-process output to take an exception path.

Interruptible Timer Intermediate Boundary Event Example

In this example, daily invoices are checked and filed. If it is first day of the month, the normal sequence flow is interrupted and the exception flow takes presidency and the invoices are prepared and paid.

The exception sequence flow returns to the normal sequence flow and invoices are filed.

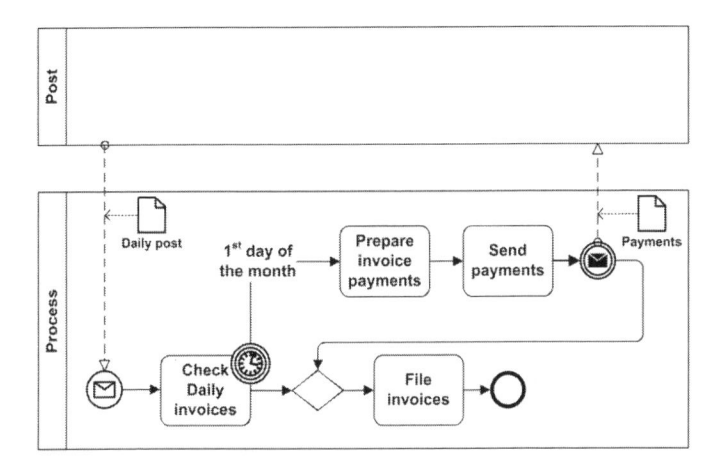

Non-Interruptible Timer Intermediate Boundary Event Example

In this example, daily invoices are checked and filed. If it is first day of the month, the normal sequence flow is not interrupted and the exception flow is used in parallel.

The exception flow prepares the invoice payments and payments are sent.

The normal sequence flow continues filing the invoices.

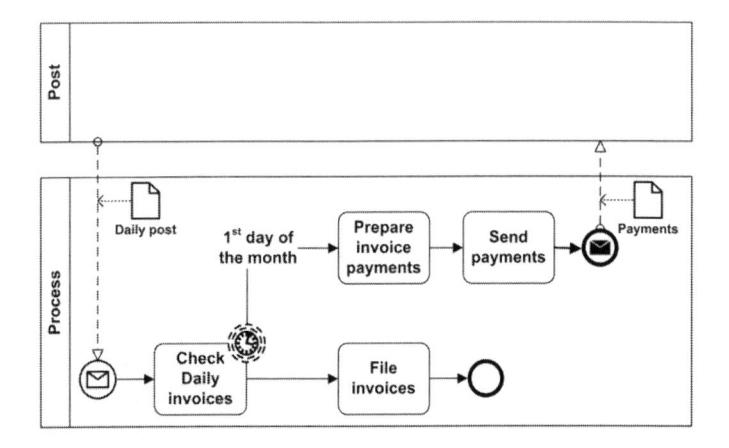

Conditional Intermediate Boundary Event

An interruptible *Conditional Intermediate Boundary Event* is depicted by two thin circles one drawn inside the other, containing a rectangle with horizontal lines.

A non-interruptible *Conditional Intermediate Boundary Event* is depicted with two thin dashed circles one drawn inside the other, containing a rectangle with horizontal lines.

A *Conditional Intermediate Boundary Event is used* as a business condition to change the normal flow into an exception flow.

Interruptible Conditional Intermediate Boundary Event Example

In this example, invoices are checked and filed. If invoices are 30 days overdue, the normal sequence flow is interrupted and the payments are prepared and paid immediately.

The exception flow returns to the normal sequence flow to file the invoices.

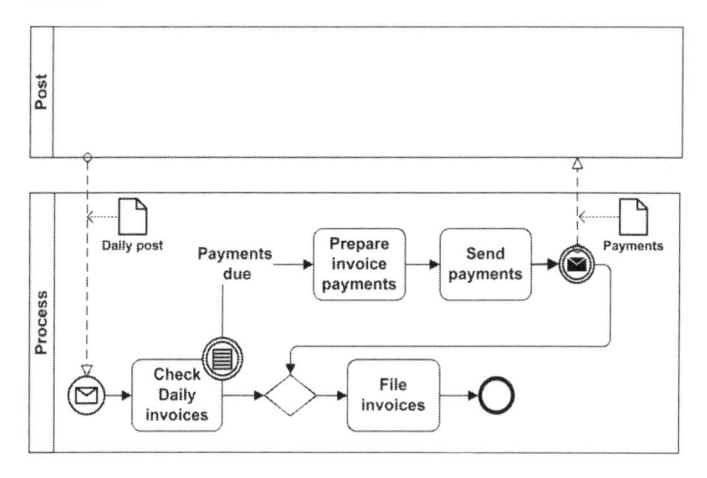

Non-Interruptible Conditional Intermediate Boundary Event Example

In this example, invoices are checked and filed. If invoices are 30 days overdue, the normal sequence flow is not interrupted but the payments are prepared and paid immediately.

The exception flow ends with payments being sent.

As the normal sequence flow is not interrupted all invoices are filed.

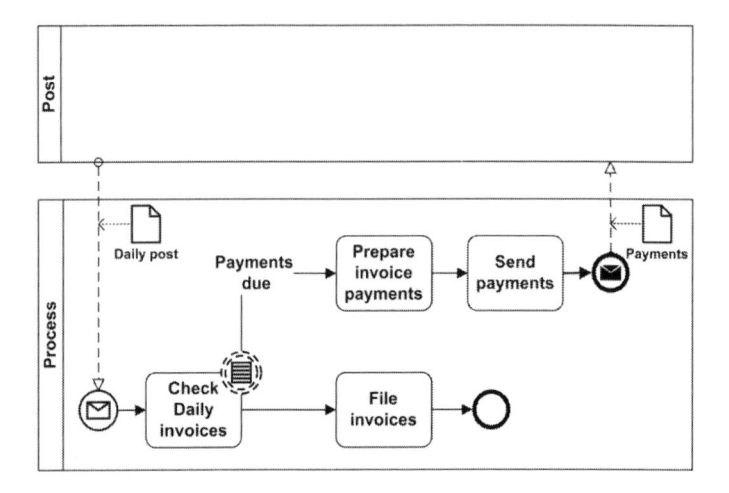

Multiple Intermediate Boundary Event

An interruptible *Multiple Intermediate Boundary Event* is depicted by two thin circles one drawn inside the other, containing an unfilled pentagon.

A non-interruptible *Multiple Intermediate Boundary Event* is depicted with two thin dashed circles one drawn inside the other, containing an unfilled pentagon.

A *Multiple Intermediate Boundary Event is* placed on the boundary of a task or sub-process to show that multiple intermediate events can trigger an exception flow.

Interruptible Multiple Intermediate Boundary Event Example

In this example, invoices are checked and filed. If invoices are 30 days overdue **OR** it is the first day of the month, the normal sequence flow is interrupted and the payments are prepared and paid immediately.

The exception flow returns to the normal sequence flow to file the invoices.

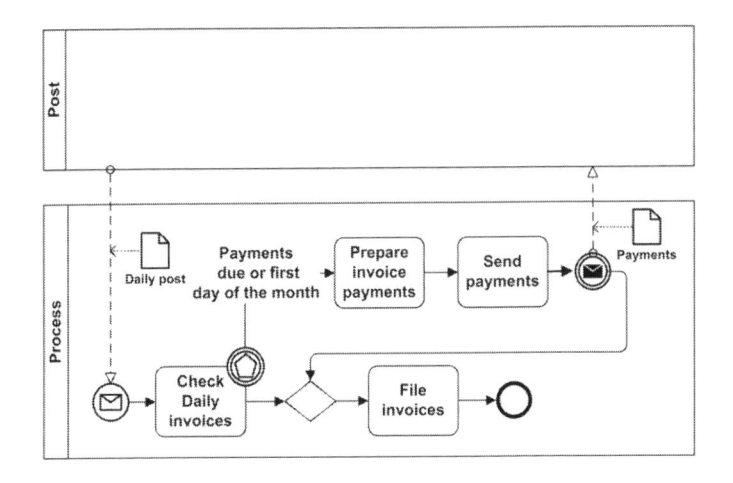

BPMN Pocket Reference 95

Non-Interruptible Multiple Intermediate Boundary Event Example

In this example, invoices are checked and filed. If invoices are 30 days overdue **OR** it is the first day of the month, the normal sequence flow is not interrupted but payments are prepared and paid immediately.

The normal sequence flow is not interrupted and the exception flow ends with payments sent while the normal sequence flow files the invoices.

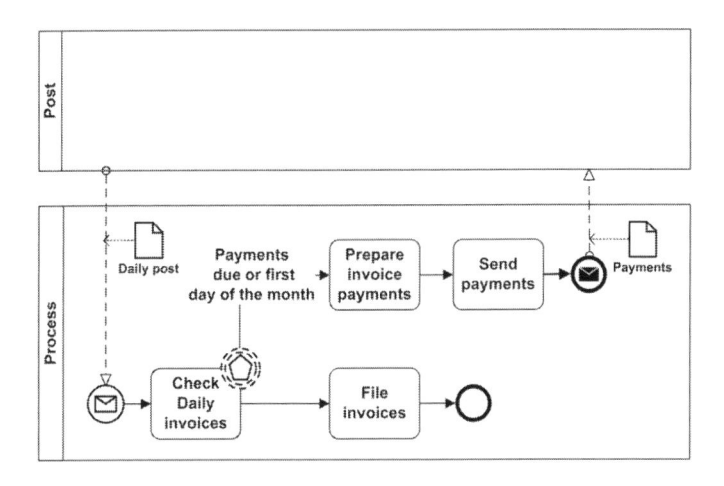

Parallel Multiple Intermediate Boundary Events

An interruptible *Parallel Multiple Intermediate Boundary Event* is depicted by two thin circles one drawn inside the other, containing an unfilled plus sign.

A non-interruptible *Parallel Multiple Intermediate Boundary E*vent is depicted by two thin dashed circles one drawn inside the other, containing an unfilled plus sign.

A *Parallel Multiple Intermediate Boundary Event* is placed on the boundary of a task or sub-process.

The exception flow is triggered when two or more different events occur simultaneously.

Interruptible Parallel Multiple Intermediate Boundary Event Example

In this example, invoices are checked and filed. If invoices are 30 days overdue **AND** it is the first day of the month the normal sequence flow is interrupted and the payments are prepared and paid immediately.

The exception flow returns to the normal sequence flow to file the invoices.

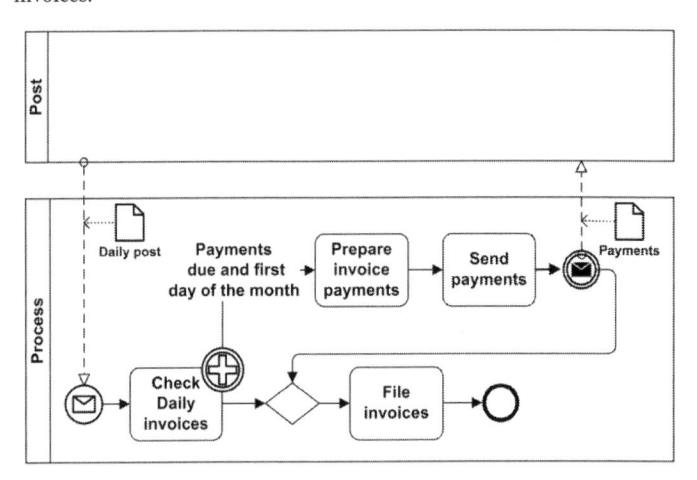

98   BPMN Pocket Reference

Non-Interruptible Parallel Multiple Intermediate Boundary Event Example

In this example, the invoices are checked and filed. If invoices are 30 days overdue **AND** it is the first day of the month, the normal sequence flow is not interrupted but payments are prepared and paid immediately.

The normal sequence flow is not interrupted and the exception flow ends with payments sent. While the normal sequence flow files the invoices.

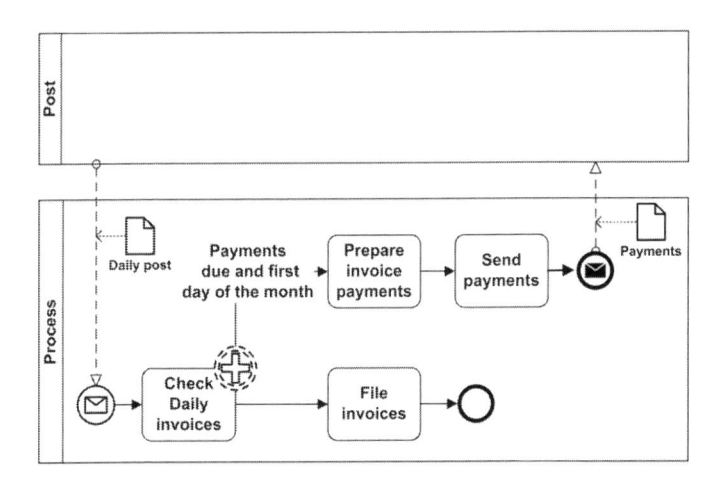

Escalation Events

Escalation Start Event

An *Escalation Start Interrupt Event* is depicted by a circle containing an upturned, unfilled arrowhead.

An *Escalation Start Non-interrupt Event* is depicted by a dashed line circle, containing an upturned, unfilled arrowhead.

Escalation Start Events cannot be used as a top level event.

*Escalation Start Event*s are only used to trigger in-line event sub-processes.

Escalation Start Events can be used as an interrupt or as a non-interrupt event in inline sub-processes, depending on the process requirements.

Escalation Intermediate Boundary Events

An *Escalation Intermediate Interrupt Boundary Event* is depicted by two thin circles one drawn inside the other, containing an unfilled, upturned arrowhead.

An *Escalation Intermediate Non-interrupt Boundary Event* is depicted by two thin circles with dashed lines one drawn inside the other, containing an unfilled, upturned arrowhead.

Escalation Intermediate Boundary Events can only be attached to the boundary of a task or sub-process.

The outgoing sequence flow or exception sequence flow is used in association with an escalation handler.

Escalation Intermediate Boundary Events can either be used as an interrupt or as a non-interrupt event in an inline sub-process, depending on the process requirements.

Escalation Intermediate Throwing Event

An *Escalation Intermediate Throwing Event* is depicted by two thin circles one drawn inside the other, containing an upturned, filled arrowhead.

An Escalation Intermediate Throwing Event is an event which is caught by an *Escalation Intermediate Boundary Event* on the edge of the nearest enclosed parent activity or sub-process.

The behaviour of the *Escalation Intermediate Throwing Event* is unspecified if it is not associated with an *Escalation Intermediate Boundary Event*.

Escalation End Event

An *Escalation End Event* is depicted by a circle drawn with a thick solid line containing an upturned, filled arrowhead.

An *Escalation End Event is a throwing event which is* caught by an *Escalation Intermediate Boundary Event* on the edge of the nearest enclosed parent activity or sub-process.

The behaviour of the *Escalation End Event* is unspecified if it is not associated with an *Escalation Intermediate Boundary Event*.

Escalation Events Example 1

A customer order is received and credit is checked.

If the customer's credit is approved, the product is shipped.

If the customer is not credit worthy, the customer records are updated and the sequence flow ends with an *Escalation End Event*.

This triggers the sub-process *Escalation Intermediate Boundary Event*, which in turn triggers the *Cancel order handler* sub-process.

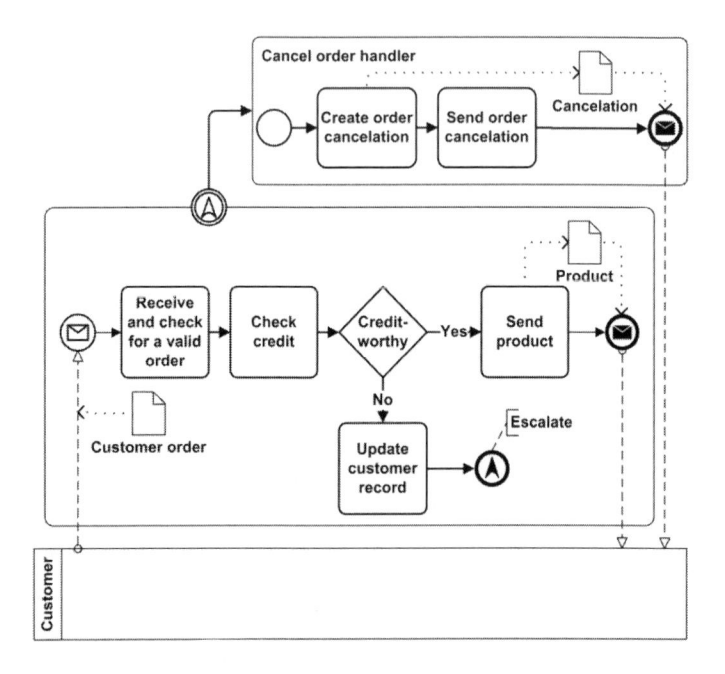

Escalation Events Example 2

A customer order is received and credit is checked.

If the customer's credit is approved, the product is shipped.

If the customer is not creditworthy, the customer records are updated and the sequence flows to an *Escalation Intermediate Throwing Event*.

The *Escalation Intermediate Throwing Event* triggers an *Intermediate Boundary Non-interrupting Event* which triggers the *Cancelation order handler* sub-process.

The *Escalation Intermediate Throwing Event* does not stop the sequence flow which continues to *Remove order entry* task, which completes the sequence.

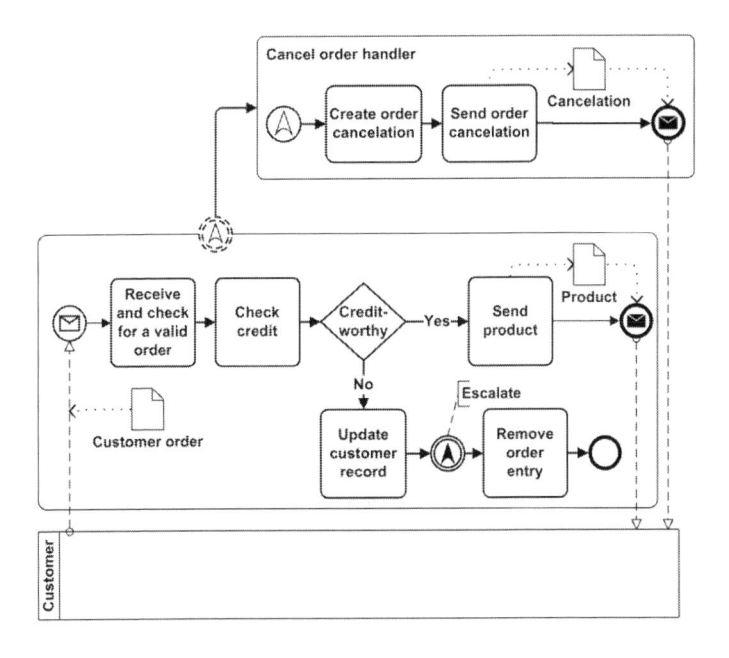

Signal Events

A *Signal Event* is used for general communication within and across process levels, pools, and between BPD's.

Signal Start Event

A *Signal Start Interrupt Event* is depicted by a circle containing an unfilled triangle.

A *Signal Start Non-interrupt Event* is depicted by a dashed line circle containing an unfilled triangle.

Signal Start Interrupt Events are used to start a top level process sequence or to start a sub-process.

Signal Start Non-interrupt Events are only used to start a sub-process.

A *Signal Start Event* is triggered by a signal throwing event from another process, which is either an *End Signal Event* or an *Intermediate Signal Throwing Event*, broadcasting a signal.

Multiple processes can have *Start Signal Events* that are triggered by the same broadcast signal throwing event.

Signal Intermediate Catching Event

A *Signal Intermediate Catching Event is depicted by* two circles one drawn inside the other, containing an unfilled triangle.

Signal Intermediate Catching Events are used for receiving signals in the same way as Signal Start Events.

Signal Intermediate Catching Events wait until a trigger arrives from a *Signal End Event* or a *Signal Intermediate Throwing Event* before starting.

Signal Intermediate Throwing Event

A *Signal Intermediate Throwing Event is depicted by* two circles one drawn inside the other, containing a filled triangle.

Signal Intermediate Throwing Events are used to send a broadcast signal while in an inline process, across process levels and pools to either a *Signal Start Event* or a *Signal Intermediate Catching Event*.

Signal End Event

A *Signal End Event is depicted by* a thick circle containing a filled triangle.

A *Signal End Event* broadcasts to any process that can receive the trigger and is sent across process levels and pools.

Signal Intermediate Event Example 1

In the following example, the monthly invoices are prepared and sent to both accounting and payment departments.

Accounting will check invoices and proceed to update their records.

After invoices have been checked the *Signal Intermediate Throwing Event* triggers the *Signal Intermediate Catching Event* to prepare payments.

When both the accounts are updated and invoices are filed, payments are sent.

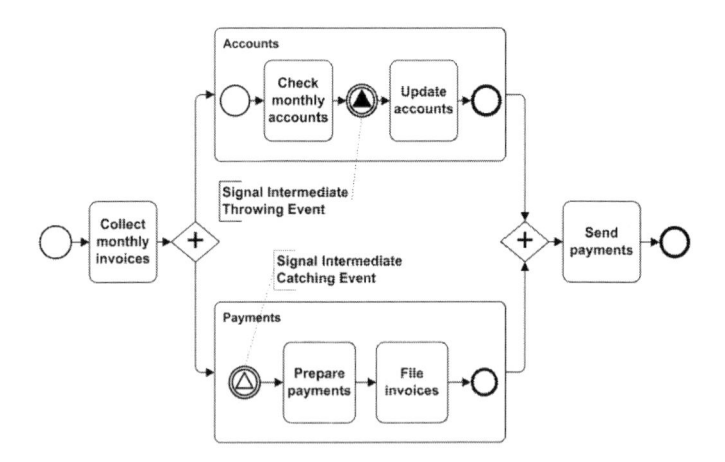

Signal Intermediate Boundary Event

A *Signal Intermediate Boundary Interrupt Event* is depicted by two thin circles one drawn inside the other, containing an unfilled triangle.

A *Signal Intermediate Boundary Non-interrupt Event* is depicted by two thin dashed circles one drawn inside the other, containing an unfilled triangle.

Signal Intermediate Boundary Events are catching events attached to the edge of an activity.

A *Signal Intermediate Boundary Event* can be triggered by *a Signal End Event* or a *Signal Intermediate Throwing Event,* which diverts the sequence flow taking the exception path.

If the *Signal Intermediate Boundary Event* is an interrupting event, the normal sequence flow ceases and the exception path is followed.

If the *Signal Intermediate Boundary Event* is a non-interrupting event, the normal sequence flow continues at the same time as the exception path.

Signal Intermediate Event Example 2

The customer's order is received and credit checked.

If the customer is creditworthy, the product is shipped, customer records are updated and a work order produced.

The sequence flow ends with a *Signal End Event* which triggers the sub-process 'Despatch product', with a *Signal Start Event*.

If the customer is not creditworthy, the exception sequence is taken and an order cancellation is produced and sent to the customer.

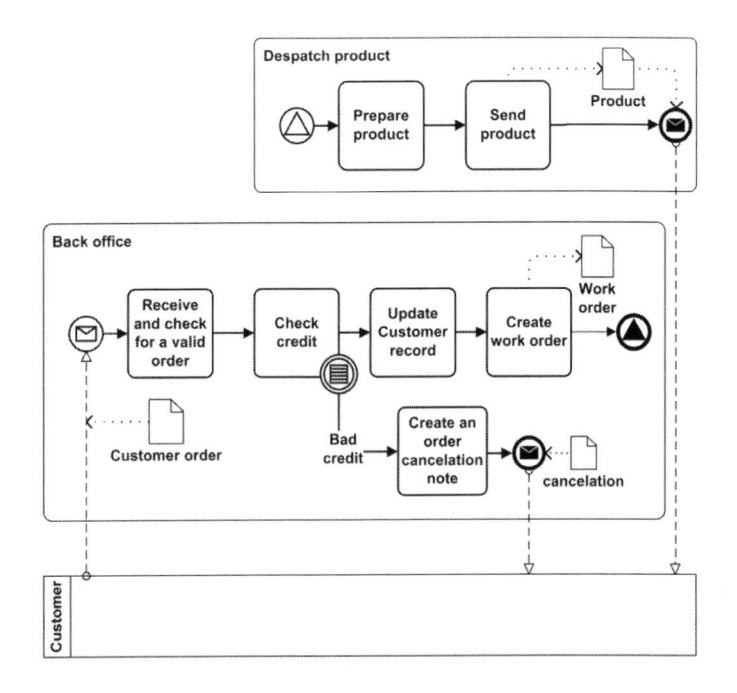

Cancel Events

Cancel End Event

A *Cancel End Event* is depicted by a thick circle containing a solid **X**.

Cancel End Events indicate that all activities in the process sequence cease immediately, including multi-Instances.

A *Cancel End Event* is a throwing event and therefore the behaviour of the process is unspecified if a *Cancel Intermediate Boundary Event* is not present.

Cancel Intermediate Boundary Event

A *Cancel Intermediate Boundary Event* is depicted by two circles containing an unfilled **X**.

A *Cancel Intermediate Boundary Event is* used only for a sub-process and is always attached to the boundary of a sub-process.

Cancel Intermediate Boundary Events are catching events triggered by the Cancel End Event within the sub-process.

Cancel Events Example

In the following example, orders are received from a customer.

The credit is checked and if the customer is creditworthy, the product is shipped.

If the customer is not creditworthy, the customer records are updated and the sequence finishes with a *Cancel End Event*.

The *Cancel End Event* is captured by a *Cancel Intermediate Boundary Event,* directing the sequence flow to a sub-process, *Handle order cancelation.*

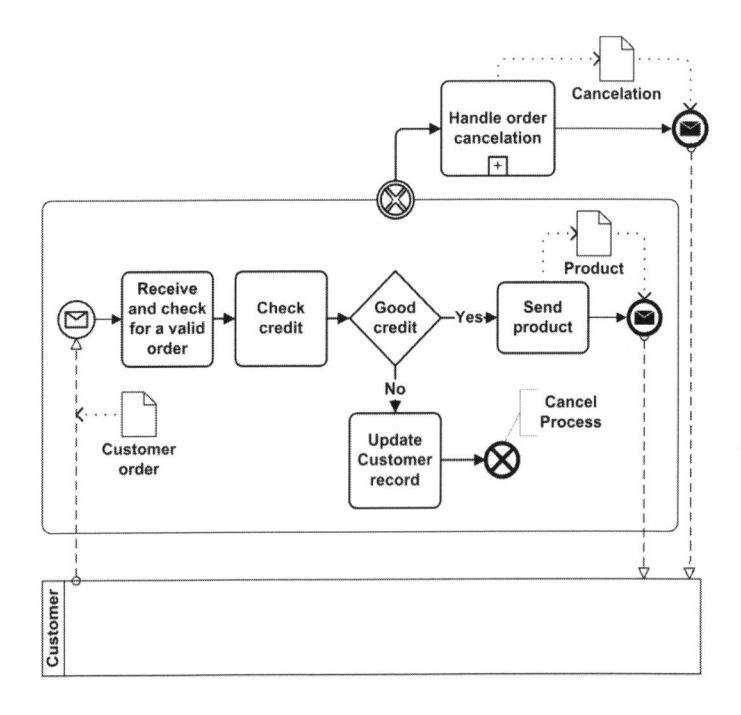

Error Events

There are three types of error events, a Start event, an Intermediate Boundary event and an End event.

An Error Event as the condition implies, is only an interrupting event.

Error Start Event

An *Error Start Event* is depicted by a circle containing an unfilled lightning marker.

An *Error Start Event* is used as an in-line event sub-process and will always interrupt the sequence flow.

Error Start Event Example

The customer's order records are checked and a cancelation order is prepared and sent to the customer.

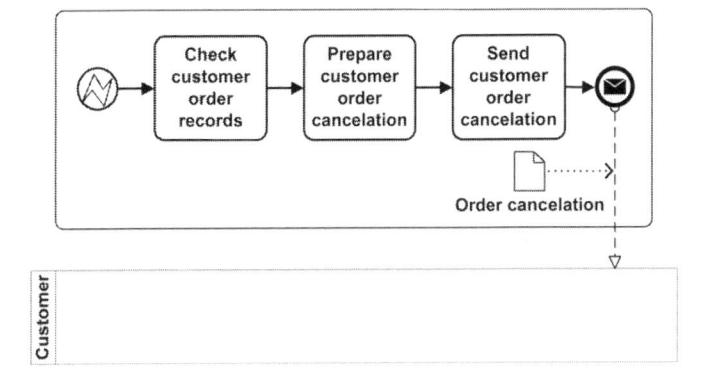

BPMN Pocket Reference

Error Intermediate Boundary Event

An Error Intermediate Boundary Event is depicted by two circles one drawn inside the other, containing an unfilled lightning marker.

Error Intermediate Boundary Events are attached to the edge of a task or sub-process to catch a specific or an unspecified error.

An *Error Intermediate Boundary Event* triggers an error handler.

Error End Event

An *Error End Event* is depicted by a thick circle containing a filled lightning marker.

An *Error End Event* is a throwing event and generates an error condition.

An error condition is caught by an *Error Intermediate Boundary Event* which is situated on the edge of a sub-process.

The behaviour of the process is unspecified if an *Error Intermediate Boundary Event* is not used.

Error Event Example 1

The customer's order is received and credit checked.

If the customer is creditworthy, the product is shipped.

If the customer is not creditworthy the sequence flow ends with an *Error End Event.*

The *Error End Event* triggers the sub-process *Error Intermediate Boundary Event,* which in turn triggers the *Handle bad credit* sub-process.

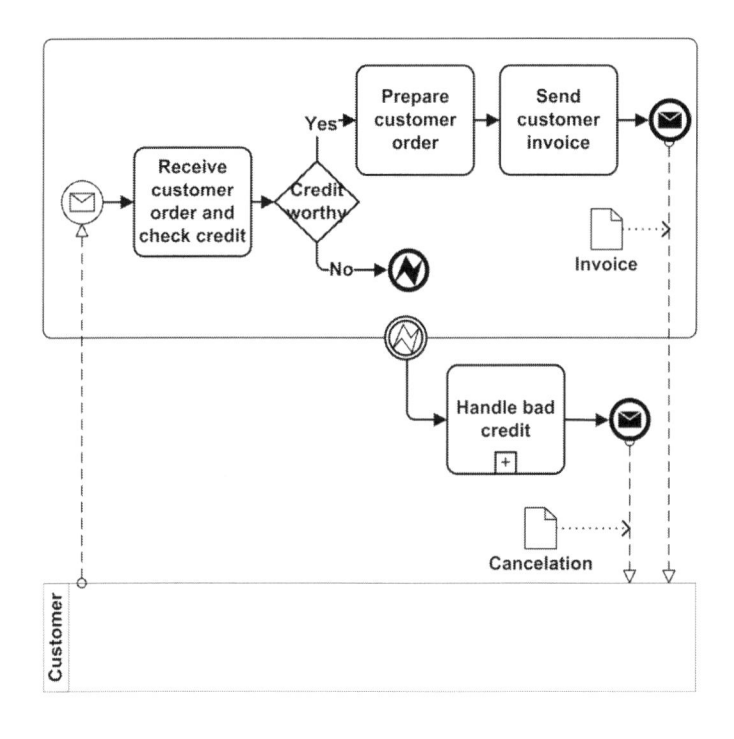

Error Event Example 2

The customer's order is received and credit checked.

If the customer is creditworthy, the product is shipped.

If the customer is not creditworthy, the *Error Intermediate Boundary Event* triggers the *Error End Event*.

The Error End Event triggers the sub-process *Error Intermediate Boundary Event,* which in turn initiates the *Handle bad credit* sub-process.

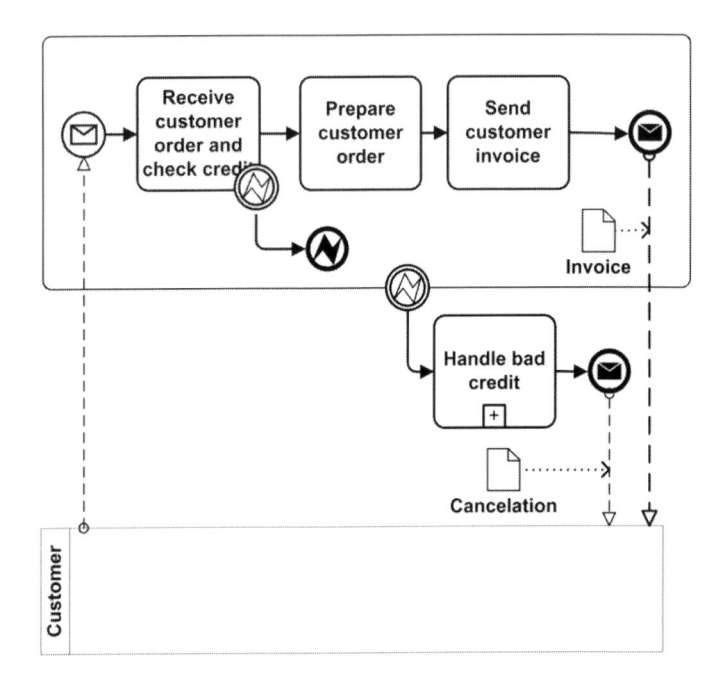

Compensation Events

Compensation is about undoing steps that were already successfully completed.

When activity results are no longer required, they need to be reversed or undone.

Compensation events undo what has already been done, in reverse order.

Note that interrupting a non-interrupting aspect of other events does not apply in the case of Compensation Events.

Compensation Start Event

A *Compensation Start Event* is depicted by a circle drawn with a thin line, containing an unfilled double triangle marker pointing left.

A *Compensation Start Event* is only used to start an in-line compensation event sub-process.

The process compensation takes place after the process has been completed and can only be triggered by the completion of the process.

Compensation Intermediate Boundary Event

A *Compensation Intermediate Boundary Event* is depicted by two thin circles one drawn inside the other, containing an unfilled double triangle marker pointing left.

Compensation Intermediate Boundary Events are attached to the edge of a task or sub-process indicating that compensation is necessary for that activity or sub-process.

Each completed activity that is subject to compensation, is compensated in the reverse order of the completion of the activities.

When a *Compensation Intermediate Boundary Event* is attached to the edge of an activity, the event is triggered by a throwing compensation event which identifies that activity or a broadcast compensation.

Compensation Activity Example

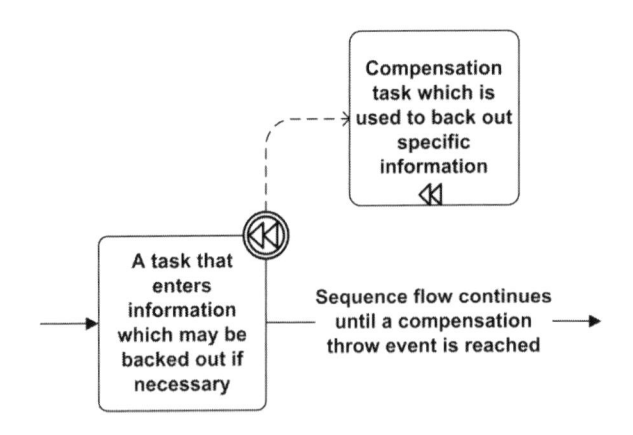

The sequence flow from a task to a compensation task is shown by a dashed line.

Compensation takes place after a Compensation Throwing Event is reached.

There is only one target activity for compensation, which cannot be a sequence of activities.

Compensation Intermediate Throwing Event

A *Compensation Intermediate Throwing Event* is depicted by two thin circles, containing a filled double triangle marker pointing left.

A *Compensation Intermediate Throwing Event* is used in a normal sequence flow and indicates that if any compensation is necessary, the compensation is executed at that time.

If the *Compensation Intermediate Throwing Event* identifies an activity, then that is the activity which will be compensated.

Compensation Intermediate Throwing Events broadcast to all activities which have been completed within the process, including the top-level process and all sub-processes.

In order to be compensated, a task or sub-process must have a Compensation Intermediate Boundary Event attached to it.

Compensation End Event Throwing

A *Compensation End Event* is depicted by a circle drawn with a thick line, containing a filled double triangle marker pointing left.

A *Compensation End Event* is an event which triggers the processing of all *Compensation Intermediate Boundary Events* in the process.

If an activity is identified in the process sequence flow which needs compensating, it is compensated.

Note that unless an activity has been identified, all activities that are completed within the process, starting with the top-level process and all sub-processes, are subject to compensation proceeding in reverse order.

Compensation End Events allow tasks or sub-processes to be "undone" using a specific compensation task or sub-process.

Compensation Example 1

In the following example, the monthly invoices are prepared and returned products are checked.

The *Compensation Intermediate Throwing Event* is an inline event and instigates compensation when necessary.

If products have been returned, invoices are nullified for these customers and invoices are not sent.

The task *Nullify invoices and update customer records* is a compensation task and prevents the customer receiving an invoice for a product that has been returned.

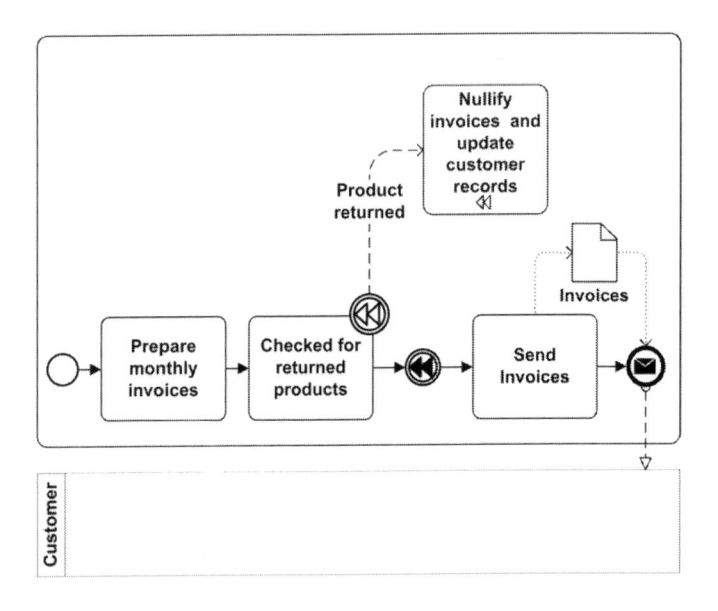

Compensation Example 2

In the following example, the monthly invoices are prepared and returned, products are checked.

The monthly invoices are prepared and the sequence flow ends with a *Compensation End Event* which triggers the *Compensation Intermediate Boundary Event*.

All invoices, where customers have returned products, are nullified by the compensation task.

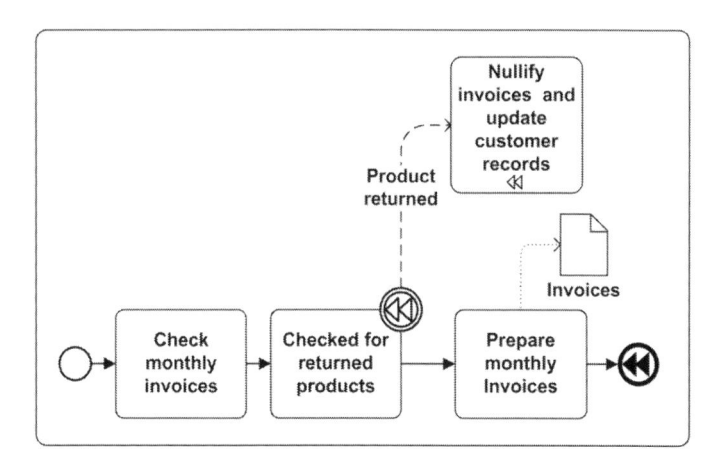

Collapsed Event Sub-Processes

Collapsed Event Sub-Processes are a specific type of sub-processes which are not triggered by normal control flows but only when the associated start event is activated.

A *Collapsed Event Sub-Process* is not part of the normal sequence flow of its parent process as there is no incoming or outgoing sequence flow.

A *Collapsed Event Sub-Process* may or may not occur while the parent process is active. However, if the parent process is active, it is possible that it will occur many times.

Unlike a standard sub-process, which uses the flow of the parent process as a trigger, a *Collapsed Event Sub-Process* has a start event with a trigger.

Each time the start event is triggered while the parent process is active, the *Collapsed Event Sub-Process* will commence.

A *Collapsed Event Sub-Process* is self-contained and not connected to the rest of the sequence flow within the sub-process.

A *Collapsed Event Sub-Process* does not have attached boundary events.

A *Collapsed Event Sub-Process* has one start event.

There are two possible consequences to the parent process when an *Event Sub-Process* is triggered

- the parent process can be interrupted
- the parent process can continue and not be interrupted

This depends on which type of start event is used.

More than one non-interrupting *Collapsed Event Sub-Processes* can be initiated at different times.

Whenever a *Collapsed Event Sub-Process* occurs it is consumed and the associated event sub-process is performed.

A *Collapsed Event Sub-Process* has the option to retrigger the event through which it was triggered, to allow the continuation outside the boundary of the associated sub-process.

All Collapsed Event Sub-Processes are depicted as a dotted line rectangle containing a plus sign (+) bottom centre.

Each Collapsed Event Sub-Process contains a specific type of start event located in the top left corner.

Message Event Sub-Processes

```
┌─────────────────┐   ┌─────────────────┐
│ ✉               │   │ ✉ (dotted)      │
│  Interrupting   │   │ Non-interrupting│
│  message event  │   │  message event  │
│  sub-process    │   │  sub-process    │
│       +         │   │       +         │
└─────────────────┘   └─────────────────┘
```

A *Message Event Sub-Process* interrupting trigger is depicted by a thin solid line circle, containing a non filled envelope.

A non-interrupting trigger is depicted by a thin dotted circle, containing a non filled envelope.

Message Event Sub-Processes are triggered by a message with the same behaviour as a receive task.

Timer Event Sub-Processes

```
┌─────────────────┐   ┌─────────────────┐
│ 🕒              │   │ 🕒 (dotted)     │
│Interrupting timer│  │ Non-interrupting│
│   event sub-    │   │  timer event sub-│
│    process      │   │     process     │
│       +         │   │       +         │
└─────────────────┘   └─────────────────┘
```

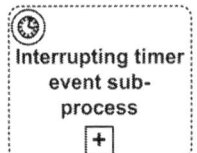

A *Timer Event Sub-Process* interrupting trigger is a thin solid line circle, containing a clock face.

A non-interrupting trigger is a thin dotted circle containing a clock face.

Timer Event Sub-Processes are triggered by a specific date and time.

BPMN Pocket Reference   121

Conditional Event Sub-Processes

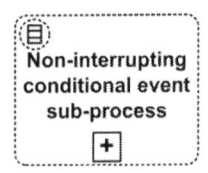

A *Conditional Event Sub-Process* interrupting trigger is depicted by a thin solid line circle, containing a rectangle with horizontal lines.

A non-interrupting trigger is depicted by a thin dotted circle, containing a rectangle with horizontal lines.

Conditional Event Sub-Processes are triggered by a specific business condition occurring.

Multiple Event Sub-Processes

A *Multiple Event Sub-Process* interrupting trigger is depicted by a thin solid line circle, containing a pentagon.

A non-interrupting trigger is depicted by a thin dotted circle, containing a pentagon.

Multiple Event Sub-Processes are triggered by receiving any combination of a message event, a timer event, a conditional event or a signal event.

Parallel Multiple Event Sub-Processes

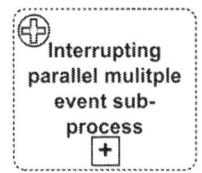

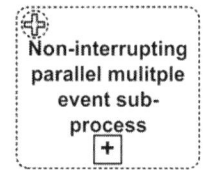

A *Parallel Multiple Event Sub-Process* interrupting trigger is depicted by a thin solid line circle, containing a non-filled plus sign.

A non-interrupting trigger is depicted by a thin dotted circle, containing a non-filled plus sign.

Multiple Event Sub-Processes are triggered by receiving any combination of a message event, a timer event, a conditional event or a signal event occurring at the same time.

Escalation Event Sub-Processes

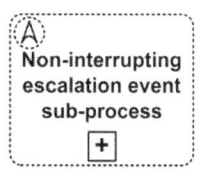

An *Escalation Event Sub-Process* interrupting trigger is depicted by a thin solid line circle, containing an upturned arrowhead.

A non-interrupting trigger is depicted by a thin dotted circle, containing an upturned arrowhead.

Escalation Event Sub-Processes are triggered by escalation throwing events.

Signal Event Sub-Processes

A *Signal Event Sub-Process* interrupting trigger is depicted by a thin solid line circle, containing a triangle.

A non-interrupting trigger is depicted by a thin dotted circle, containing a triangle.

Signal Event Sub-Processes are triggered by a throwing signal event from another process.

Error Event Sub-Process

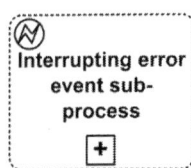

An *Error Event Sub-Process* has an interrupting trigger depicted by a thin solid line circle, containing an unfilled lightning marker.

An *Error Event Sub-Process* is triggered by a throwing error event from another process.

Compensation Event Sub-Process

A *Compensation Event Sub-Process* has an interrupting trigger depicted by a thin solid line circle, containing an unfilled double triangle, pointing left.

A *Compensation Event Sub-Process* is triggered by a throwing compensation event from another process.

Further Reading

For further reading and understanding of business processes and BPMN the following books are recommended:

BPMN Modeling and Reference Guide by Stephen White and Derek Miers.
ISBN 978-0-9777527-2-0
BPMN Method & Style by Bruce Silver
ISBN 978-0-9823681-0-7

Kenneth Sherry is also the author of '**Insight Into Business Processes**'. The book gives a clear and comprehensive overview of business processes for those who are seeking an insight in today's modern business process management.

The following is an overview of some of the topics covered in 'Insight Into Business Processes'.

- Business process management
- Business process modelling
- Business rules
- Gathering business process requirements
- Business process documentation
- Business process fulfilment staff procedures
- The role of the business process analyst

You are invited to send comments and useful improvements to enhance this reference book for future editions.

Kenneth J Sherry

www.admaks.com
kenneth@admaks.com

Printed in Great Britain
by Amazon.co.uk, Ltd.,
Marston Gate.